TEXTBOOKS IN ACADEMIC LIBRARIES

AN ALCTS MONOGRAPH

TEXTBOOKS IN ACADEMIC LIBRARIES

Selection, Circulation, and Assessment

EDITED BY CHRIS DIAZ

ala
editions

An imprint of the American Library Association

CHICAGO 2017

CHRIS DIAZ is the digital publishing services librarian at Northwestern University (Evanston, Illinois), where he manages the institutional repository and the library's digital publishing program. He became interested in college textbooks and open educational resources when he was the collections management librarian at National Louis University (Chicago).

© 2017 by the American Library Association

Extensive effort has gone into ensuring the reliability of the information in this book; however, the publisher makes no warranty, express or implied, with respect to the material contained herein.

ISBNS
978-0-8389-1587-5 (paper)
978-0-8389-1602-5 (PDF)
978-0-8389-1603-2 (ePub)
978-0-8389-1604-9 (Kindle)

Library of Congress Cataloging-in-Publication Data

Names: Diaz, Chris, 1988- editor.
Title: Textbooks in academic libraries : selection, circulation, and assessment / edited by Chris Diaz.
Description: Chicago : ALA Editions, an imprint of the American Library Association, 2017. | Series: An ALCTS monograph | Includes bibliographical references.
Identifiers: LCCN 2017014886| ISBN 9780838915875 (pbk. : alk. paper) | ISBN 9780838916025 (pdf) | ISBN 9780838916032 (epub) | ISBN 9780838916049 (Kindle)
Subjects: LCSH: Academic libraries—Collection development. | Libraries—Special collections—College textbooks. | Academic libraries—Reserve collections. | Academic libraries—Circulation and loans. | College textbooks—Prices—United States. | Academic libraries—United States—Case studies.
Classification: LCC Z675.U5 T454 2017 | DDC 025.2/1877—dc23 LC record available at https://lccnloc.gov/2017014886.

Cover design by Alejandra Diaz.

Text composition by Dianne M. Rooney in the Adobe Caslon Pro and Archer typefaces.

♾ This paper meets the requirements of ANSI/NISO Z39.48–1992 (Permanence of Paper).

Printed in the United States of America

21 20   19   18   17   5   4   3   2   1

CONTENTS

Contents

INTRODUCTION

Chris Diaz

No matter how you look at it, college is expensive. The average cost of one year of college in 2013 was over $20,000, a fivefold increase from thirty years earlier.[1] Year after year, higher education costs have been increasing at higher rates than almost everything else in the United States. Even after subtracting grants and scholarships, the net cost of attendance for students exceeded increases in the Consumer Price Index by over 20 percent between 2001 and 2012, a trend that is continuing.[2] There is currently an aggregate student debt balance of over one trillion dollars.[3] Meanwhile, student enrollment is stagnant, if not declining, despite increasing demands of the job market for college degree holders.[4] The cost burden and the need for higher education is felt so widely across North America that it has brought college affordability to the forefront of the conversation about higher education, putting stress on campus administrators, governments, and the general public to find solutions.

College textbook prices have risen in tandem with these larger costs and are part of the day-to-day concern over college affordability among students. College textbook prices rose 82 percent between 2002 and 2012, following similar increases in published tuition and fees rates during the same time period.[5] This reality has mobilized student advocacy groups and industry analysts to study consumer behavior in the college textbook marketplace. The Student Public Interest Research Groups (Student PIRGS) reports that 30 percent of undergraduate students use financial aid to pay for textbooks, and 65 percent decide against buying a textbook because they cannot afford it.[6] Students in community colleges, nonselective universities, or from low-income households are disproportionately affected by high college textbook prices, placing them more at risk for course failure and dropping out. These students are also more likely to either use student loans to buy textbooks or not purchase the textbook at all.[7] The prevalence of this burden is echoed in a Nielsen report of a national survey, which found that "students are very selective in acquiring course materials because of limited budgets," leading a significant percentage of students to download course materials illegally from file-sharing websites or go without them.[8]

These reports and findings should not be surprising to academic librarians. The demand for free or affordable college textbooks can be heard from a variety of positions: public services librarians field these questions near the beginning of each term, interlibrary loan departments fill or reject innumerable textbook requests, collection development librarians balance this demand against increasing serials costs and the need to build scholarly collections, and campus administrators grapple with academic freedom concerns over textbook selection from faculty. Libraries are committed to creating a positive and equitable learning experience, but it would be unwise if not impossible for them to buy and circulate every textbook needed at a college or university for all students. There are good reasons for libraries to avoid these materials altogether: college textbooks are expensive and new editions are published every few years; textbooks are not scholarly; and textbooks have traditionally been the student's responsibility to purchase, not the library's responsibility.[9] Yet, academic libraries have been collecting textbooks for over a decade and continue to do so with more impact than ever.[10]

Consider the demand for college textbooks on your campus in the context of your library's monographic circulation trends. Total circulation between the 1990s and the 2010s has declined by nearly a third.[11] This trend is echoed throughout this book, except in the cases where the book is assigned as a textbook.

What can we learn from over a decade of experience collecting college textbooks? This collection of case studies pulls together creative approaches and best practices for formalizing, promoting, and managing print textbook reserve programs. (A textbook reserve is a collection of required course materials that do not circulate outside the library building.) Among many others, this book provides answers to the following questions:

- How can textbook reserves contribute to campus recruitment and retention efforts?
- How can textbook reserves assist with library outreach to students and faculty?

- How will implementing textbook reserves affect staffing and workflows?
- How can we work with the campus bookstore to provide textbook reserves?
- How can we budget for long-term textbook reserve programs?
- What can we learn from analyzing textbook circulation data?

Throughout this book, particular attention is given to budgeting, supporting institutional priorities (such as student recruitment, retention, and success), and sustainability.

The anxiety of purchasing college textbooks is part of the larger issue of college affordability. Students, parents, financial officers, and campus administrators are looking for ways to bring the cost of attendance down, and this book demonstrates how the library can serve these interests through textbook reserve programs. Textbook reserves bring students into the library and can introduce them to the range of services that libraries provide. If you're considering building a textbook program, or have one but are interested in new insight for increasing the efficiency of your workflows or impact on campus, these case studies will help you collect and manage college textbooks.

Notes

1. National Center for Education Statistics, Fast Facts, "Tuition Costs of College and Universities," http://nces.ed.gov/fastfacts/display.asp?id=76. The "fivefold increase" in tuition costs is adjusted for inflation over the thirty-year period.
2. Adam Stoll, David H. Bradley, and Shannon Mahan, "Overview of the Relationship between Federal Student Aid and Increases in College Prices," Congressional Research Service, Washington, DC, UNT Digital Library, http://digital.library.unt.edu/ark:/67531/metadc811913/.
3. David P. Smole, "A Snapshot of Student Loan Debt," *In Focus* (March 2015), Congressional Research Service, Washington, DC, UNT Digital Library, http://digital.library.unt.edu/ark:/67531/metadc819639/.
4. For enrollment stagnation data, see Table 302.60 from "Digest of Education Statistics," National Center for Education Statistics, https://nces.ed.gov/programs/digest/d16/tables/dt16_302.60.asp. According to the Center on Education and the Workforce at Georgetown University, "in 1973, workers with postsecondary education held only 28 percent of jobs; by comparison, they held 59 percent of jobs in 2010 and will hold 65 percent of jobs in 2020"; from Anthony P. Carnevale, Nicole Smith, and Jeff Strohl,

"Recovery: Job Growth and Education Requirements through 2020," available at https://cew.georgetown.edu/cew-reports/recovery-job-growth-and-education -requirements-through-2020/.

5. United States Government Accountability Office, "College Textbooks: Students Have Greater Access to Textbook Information" (June 2013), GAO-13–368, www.gao.gov/ assets/660/655066.pdf.

6. Ethan Senack and Robert Donoghue, "Covering the Cost," Student Public Interest Research Group, published February 2, 2016, www.studentpirgs.org/reports/sp/ covering-cost; Ethan Senack, "Fixing the Broken Textbook Market," Student Public Research Interest Group, published January 27, 2014, www.uspirg.org/reports/usp/ fixing-broken-textbook-market.

7. Senack and Donoghue, "Covering the Cost"; and Senack, "Fixing the Broken Textbook Market."

8. Nielsen Company, "Textbook Trends: How U.S. College Students Source Course Materials," *Insights,* published August 18, 2016, www.nielsen.com/us/en/insights/ news/2016/textbook-trends-how-us-college-students-source-course-materials.html.

9. Rick Anderson, "Academic Libraries and the Textbook Taboo: Is It Time to Get Over It?" *The Scholarly Kitchen* (blog), published July 7, 2016, https://scholarlykitchen.sspnet .org/2016/07/07/academic-libraries-and-the-textbook-taboo-time-to-get-over-it/; Cynthia Hsieh and Rhonelle Runner, "Textbooks, Leisure Reading, and the Academic Library," *Library Collections, Acquisitions, and Technical Services* 29, no. 2 (2005), http:// dx.doi.org/10.1016/j.lcats.2005.04.005.

10. Mary S. Laskowski, "The Textbook Problem: Investigating One Possible Solution," *Library Collections, Acquisitions, and Technical Services* 31, no. 3-4 (2007), http://dx.doi .org/10.1016/j.lcats.2007.09.001.

11. Rick Anderson, "Print on the Margins: Circulation Trends in Major Research Libraries," *Library Journal* (blog), published June 2, 2011, http://lj.libraryjournal.com/ 2011/06/academic-libraries/print-on-the-margins-circulation-trends-in-major -research-libraries/.

Bibliography

Anderson, Rick. "Academic Libraries and the Textbook Taboo: Is It Time to Get Over It?" *The Scholarly Kitchen* (blog). Published July 7, 2016. https://scholarlykitchen.sspnet. org/2016/07/07/academic-libraries-and-the-textbook-taboo-time-to-get-over-it/.

———. "Print on the Margins: Circulation Trends in Major Research Libraries." *Library Journal* (blog). Published June 2, 2011. http://lj.libraryjournal.com/2011/06/academic -libraries/print-on-the-margins-circulation-trends-in-major-research-libraries/.

Carnevale, Anthony P., Nicole Smith, and Jeff Strohl. "Recovery: Job Growth and Education Requirements through 2020." Center on Education and the Workforce at Georgetown University. https://cew.georgetown.edu/ccw-reports/recovery-job-growth-and-education-requirements-through-2020/.

Hsieh, Cynthia, and Rhonell Runner. "Textbooks, Leisure Reading, and the Academic Library." *Library Collections, Acquisitions, and Technical Services* 29, no. 2 (2005): 192–204. http://dx.doi.org/10.1016/j.lcats.2005.04.005.

Laskowski, Mary S. "The Textbook Problem: Investigating One Possible Solution." *Library Collections, Acquisitions, and Technical Services* 31, no. 3-4 (2007): 161–70. http://dx.doi.org/10.1016/j.lcats.2007.09.001.

National Center for Education Statistics. "Digest of Education Statistics." Table 302.60. https://nccs.ed.gov/programs/digest/d16/tables/dt16_302.60.asp.

———. "Tuition Costs of College and Universities." Fast Facts. http://nces.ed.gov/fastfacts/display.asp?id-76.

Nielsen Company. "Textbook Trends: How U.S. College Students Source Course Materials." *Insights* (blog). Published August 18, 2016. www.nielsen.com/us/en/insights/news/2016/textbook-trends-how-us-college-students-source-course-materials.html.

Senack, Ethan. "Fixing the Broken Textbook Market." Student Public Research Interest Group. Published January 27, 2014. www.uspirg.org/reports/usp/fixing-broken-textbook-market.

Senack, Ethan, and Robert Donoghue. "Covering the Cost." Student Public Interest Research Group. Published February 2, 2016. www.studentpirgs.org/reports/sp/covering-cost.

Smole, David P. "A Snapshot of Student Loan Debt." *In Focus.* March 2015. Congressional Research Service. Washington, DC. UNT Digital Library. http://digital.library.unt.edu/ark:/67531/metadc819639/.

Stoll, Adam, David H. Bradley, and Shannon Mahan. "Overview of the Relationship between Federal Student Aid and Increases in College Prices." Congressional Research Service. Washington, DC. UNT Digital Library. http://digital.library.unt.edu/ark:/67531/metadc811913/.

United States Government Accountability Office. "College Textbooks: Students Have Greater Access to Textbook Information." June 2013. GAO-13–368. www.gao.gov/assets/660/655066.pdf.

1

"BASICALLY EVERYTHING I NEED, I KNOW THE LIBRARY HAS IT"

A Case Study of SUNY Canton's Textbook Program

Rachel A. Koenig and Cori Wilhelm

Concerns surrounding textbook affordability are on the rise and receiving increased scrutiny by students, librarians, and faculty. A chart produced by the U.S. Bureau of Labor Statistics indicates that the price of textbooks has increased 945 percent since 1978, while the prices of medical care (604 percent), new homes (408 percent), and overall inflation (262 percent) have seen significantly less growth.[1] The future of academia is affected by this exponential growth. It is becoming apparent that the increase in the price of textbooks has a significant and negative impact on student academic success and college retention. While modern-day students are savvy shoppers—renting textbooks, shopping online, or sharing with peers—the burden of spending thousands of dollars on course materials remains a significant problem for many.

Because textbook affordability affects students' satisfaction, academic success, and retention, academic librarians must take an active role in addressing this critical student need. Providing textbook reserves—a collection of required course materials that do not circulate outside the library building—is one strategy academic libraries are using to increase access and contribute to retention. This chapter serves as an in-depth case study of the implementation and evolution of the textbook reserve program at the State University of New York College of Technology at Canton (SUNY Canton) and students' perceptions of its impact on their success and retention. The chapter concludes with a discussion of plans for the program's evolution and plans to engage the institution's faculty and administration.

LITERATURE REVIEW

Literature about libraries and textbook reserves intensified in the mid-2000s; however, libraries have provided students with access to textbook collections since the nineteenth century.[2] Much of the early literature emphasizes the limited scope of textbook reserve collections despite the growing concern about textbook affordability.[3] However, with steadily rising costs, students are increasingly dependent on libraries to carry the titles they need for class. As a result, articles examining librarian implementation of textbook collections appear to be on the rise, and the trend is becoming increasingly controversial.

There are multiple reasons why academic librarians forbid the acquisition of textbooks for both reserve and circulating collections. In their examination of library collection policies, Hsieh and Runner found that the majority of libraries do not collect textbooks due to high cost, processing time, rapid obsolescence, and the need to purchase alternative curriculum materials.[4] The same findings were reported in a study by Pollitz and Christie, who added space concerns to that list, while Laura Kane McElfresh noted that transactions at her library's reserve desk were excessively labor-intensive and could not be sustained.[5] No doubt, these findings represent occurrences at many academic libraries across the nation and are important variables to keep in mind when considering the practicality of textbook reserves.

The attitudes of academic library employees additionally explain why libraries take a "no textbook" approach to collection development. Bonnie Imler believes students feel a sense of entitlement and are surprised when the library does not have their textbooks. Instead, Imler argues that it is solely the student's responsibility to purchase these materials.[6] Other librarian authors take a more philosophical approach to their dislike of textbook reserves. While these librarians understand the economic constraints associated with rising textbook prices, they do not believe textbook reserves are the solution. In fact, they believe textbook reserves are part of the problem. Donald A. Barclay admits that for a student who cannot afford textbooks, a library's copy is better than no textbook at all; however, he believes that faculty "have been disincentivized from taking serious, concerted action about textbook costs thanks, in part, to the textbook reserve systems."[7] Barclay's thoughts are echoed in a plethora of blog posts hoping to raise awareness about open educational resources (OERs).[8] These writers believe that libraries should advocate for free OERs and reject textbook reserves as the best and most empowering solutions to the textbook affordability crisis.

On the other hand, a number of libraries and librarians believe textbooks belong in an academic library's collection. As noted above, many libraries do not collect textbooks on account of the rapid obsolescence of their content and libraries' inability to purchase new editions each year. A number of studies prove, however, that reserve textbooks circulate far more than books in the regular collection.[9] In 2007 Caroline Crouse analyzed the textbook collection at the University of Minnesota and discovered that "the average [reserve textbook] circulated 3.8 times over the three semesters [of the project's duration] while the average text in the library collection circulates 2.5 times over its lifetime."[10] Crouse's findings are upheld in an opinion piece by McDonald and Burke in *American Libraries.* The authors note that textbooks will most likely receive higher circulation numbers than items housed in the permanent collection for decades, and will do so before those editions become obsolete.[11]

While there are practical reasons for collecting textbooks, other librarians focus on a "user-centered" mission. An opinion piece about textbooks, written by McDonald and Burke, tasks librarians to "reasonably respond to expressed needs for materials as we develop our collections."[12] In doing so, libraries fulfill their central mission to provide information and materials for learning. Middlemas, Morrison, and Farina-Hess responded to McDonald and Burke with a reexamination of Grossmont College Library's collection development and reserves policies to include the collection of textbooks. In doing so, the authors found that student and faculty satisfaction with library services rose, noting that "students get what they want most from the library, faculty is appreciative of the service, and the library's image has correspondingly improved."[13] Jeremy Sayles, another librarian author, argues in favor of categorizing textbooks as books or monographs when making collection development decisions. Sayles notes that "perhaps we should pay attention to our libraries' information needs rather than to some label that has been affixed to a resource."[14]

SUNY Canton's Southworth Library Learning Commons (SLLC) recognizes the complexities of textbooks, textbook reserve collections, and their debated effects on library sustainability. It is at the core of the SLLC mission to prioritize access for students in an effort to aid retention. The following study examines students' perspectives concerning SUNY Canton's textbook program in an attempt to garner enhanced attention for the financial issues faced by our specific student body. Librarians at SLLC hope to meet students' needs, including their academic success, by providing a robust textbook collection while pressing needed reforms concerning the textbook crisis.

THE SOUTHWORTH LIBRARY LEARNING COMMONS TEXTBOOK PROGRAM

SUNY Canton is one of sixty-four state-operated campuses in the extensive State University of New York system. One of seven colleges of technology within the system, SUNY Canton awards one-year certificate, two-year associate, and four-year bachelor degrees in applied fields such as criminal justice, business, engineering technologies, and nursing. The student body during the 2015–16 academic year was composed of approximately 3,200 students, 26 percent of whom identify as a race or ethnicity other than Caucasian. Twenty-seven percent of students are nontraditional college age, 66 percent are economically disadvantaged, and 46 percent are first-generation college students. This diverse student body represents underserved student populations, many of whom cannot afford rising education and textbook costs.

The college's access-driven mission prioritizes student support services, and the library's textbook program is one of many existing and developing retention efforts. With these efforts in mind, the library director, with the full support of the dean of academic support services, intentionally earmarks part of the library's annual budget for reserve textbook purchases, separate from and in addition to the general acquisitions budget. While the textbook allocation represents only 6 percent of the library's acquisitions budget, the impact of the reserve textbook program is considerable. Besides direct purchases, the other primary source of textbook acquisition is donations. Donations are solicited via e-mail and strategically placed drop boxes. Faculty donate both desk and personal copies of many textbooks. Students also donate dozens of books each semester, often choosing to do so rather than sell them back for inadequate prices.

Given this limited budget, SLLC librarians must prioritize which books can be purchased each semester. When reviewing the list of textbooks adopted for use, considerations such as cost and number of students enrolled in the course help to determine which books are purchased. For example, prioritized courses are those with multiple sections or with enrollments over thirty students, and very inexpensive textbooks (such as those priced under $20) are not considered. The reserves librarian purchases textbooks in stages, and can reevaluate and reprioritize the potential purchase list throughout the process. By targeting those titles that will provide the most positive financial impact for the most students, the librarians select approximately 80 titles to purchase each semester, with approximately 50 additional titles acquired through donation. The textbook collection currently includes approximately 70 percent of textbooks for 100-level courses, which typically have the highest student enrollment.

To increase the awareness of the textbook reserve collection, SLLC uses various strategies to market the program to both new and returning students. The textbook collection is highlighted during admissions tours for prospective students and families, and tour guides often underscore their own use of the program along with the potential cost savings. Other avenues of student-focused communication include campus e-mail, a monthly digital newsletter, digital and print signage in the building, and social media posts.

Each semester, the reserves librarian uses the LibGuides content management system to post a public Google spreadsheet containing a list of current textbook holdings. Using this method, the current semester's textbook list can be frequently updated with an indication of which titles the library owns. Though the textbook reserves are cataloged and searchable within the library's online discovery service, statistics and feedback from students suggest the LibGuide is a heavily used and appreciated resource.

The textbook program at SLLC has steadily increased in popularity and student use, and SLLC librarians recognize instances of student dissatisfaction with textbook costs and use in their courses. In an effort to maintain and grow the collection and meet the demands of SUNY Canton students, SLLC librarians assessed the program's impact on student satisfaction and retention. The following methodology and findings showcase research efforts at SLLC that may be replicated at other institutions facing similar student discontent.

Methods

The study was conducted in three parts. The first portion of the study examined the existing textbook reserve program at SLLC to determine its potential financial savings for students. To accomplish this task, the reserves librarian first gathered statistics from the Aleph circulation module to compare circulation figures between the reserve collection and the library's overall non-reserve collection. The highest-circulating reserve textbooks were identified for a projected cost analysis, which is discussed in the findings below. Using the institution's course offerings, projected course enrollments, and textbook list prices, the librarian extrapolated potential savings per course and per student.

The examination of the textbook program was supported by a nineteen-question online survey designed by the assessment and reserves librarians at SLLC. The survey was approved by SUNY Canton's Institutional Review Board and was created using LibGuides. The anonymous survey was dispersed to all SUNY Canton students via a campus e-mail discussion list as well as word of mouth. Other marketing efforts included a call for participants in the library's newsletter and in a digital campus-wide weekly newsletter. In developing the survey questionnaire, the librarians took inspiration from the Florida Student Textbook Survey, which was replicated at Buffalo State University. Several questions were adopted and supplemented with targeted inquiries concerning students' usage of SLLC and its textbook reserves collection.

Finally, the assessment and reserves librarians organized a series of five focus groups to expand the conversation about the textbook program and gather feedback from students. An e-mailed electronic flyer invited students to participate in focus group meetings. Focus group questions prompted students to comment on decisions made concerning textbook purchases, whether the library—including textbook reserves—impacted their academic success, and to provide thoughts about the library or textbooks. The librarians hoped to gather enough anecdotal evidence to determine whether the textbook program at SLLC had a positive effect on retention at SUNY Canton.

The survey was open for four weeks in April and May 2016, and focus groups met during the last three weeks of the academic year. LibWizard, the assessment tool associated with LibGuides, was used to analyze the survey results while the reserves librarian transcribed conversations recorded during focus groups. The two librarians came together to interpret the findings, which follow.

Findings and Discussion

Circulation Statistics

Due to managerial decisions, expanded resources and services, and targeted marketing, patron traffic in the library drastically increased between 2008 and 2015. This, along with a growing awareness of the textbook reserve program, drove the circulation of textbooks steadily upward during the same time period.

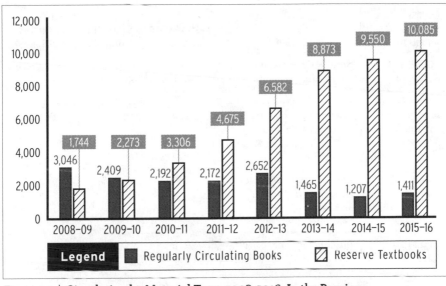

Figure 1.1 | **Circulation by Material Type, 2008-2016: In the Previous Two Years, Textbooks Circulated over Seven Times More Than Non-Reserve Print Books**

In contrast, the circulation of regular print books steadily decreased as the trend toward electronic resources shifted library acquisitions and students' use accordingly. Similar to the findings by Caroline Crouse (noted above), the circulation of reserve textbooks at SLLC has surpassed that of non-reserve print books every year since 2010 (figure 1.1). In fact, many non-reserve print books did not circulate whatsoever, while some individual textbooks were checked out over 1,000 times.

When determining the financial impact of the textbook program on the student body, the researchers considered textbook costs, program requirements, and course enrollments. If every student in a course were to use the SLLC textbook reserves rather than purchase the textbook individually, the potential cost savings for certain high-enrollment courses would be over $25,000 per course (figure 1.2), a significant figure for a small college. Approximate prices of new textbooks purchased at the SUNY Canton bookstore were used to determine the potential savings.

On a more personal scale, a typical student could save hundreds of dollars per semester by using the program. As shown in figure 1.3, the textbook reserve program would save an incoming freshman in the business, accounting, and finance majors at SUNY Canton $773 in their first semester. The potential

COURSE NUMBER AND NAME	TEXTBOOK	APPROXIMATE COST ($)	STUDENTS ENROLLED	POTENTIAL SAVINGS FOR COURSE ($)
MATH 111 – Survey of Math	*Survey of Mathematics* – Angel and Runde (Pearson)	165	170	28,050
MATH 106 – Intermediate Algebra	*Intermediate Algebra for College Students* – Angel, Abbot, and Runde (Pearson)	215	395	84,925
ACCT 101 – Introduction to Accounting	*Financial & Managerial Accounting* – Warren and Reeve (Cengage Learning)	290	265	76,850
CHEM 101 – Introduction to Chemistry	*Introductory Chemistry: A Foundation* – Zumdahl and DeCoste (Brooks Cole)	215	120	25,800
BSAD 201 – Business Law	*Business Law* – Cheeseman (Pearson)	230	210	48,300

Figure 1.2 | **Potential Savings per Course of Print Textbooks on Reserve**

COURSE	COURSE NAME	TEXTBOOK TITLE	APPROXIMATE COST ($)	DOES THE LIBRARY HAVE?
ACCT 101	Foundations of Financial Accounting	*Financial & Managerial Accounting*	303	YES
BSAD 100	Introduction to Business	*Contemporary Business*	176	YES
ECON 101	Macroeconomics	*Econ Macro 4*	70	YES
ENGL 101	Expository Writing	Varies by faculty – EX: *Everything's an Argument with Readings*	68	Varies
FYEP 101	First Year Experience	No book	—	
MATH 111	Survey of Mathematics	*Survey of Mathematics*	156	YES
		TOTAL	$773	

Figure 1.3 | **Potential Savings for a First-Semester Freshman in Business**

savings of the textbook program is staggering, and feedback from survey and focus group respondents highlights the significant value of the program and its impact on student success.

Survey and Focus Group Findings

Ninety-seven students completed the survey, which consisted of both open- and close-ended questions. The survey experienced a fairly even response rate among students in their first through fifth years of study at SUNY Canton. The majority of students (56 percent) were between the ages of 18 and 21, and 27 percent of respondents were nontraditional college age, an accurate representation of SUNY Canton's student body. Students who completed the survey were heavy textbook users. Eighty-eight percent purchased textbooks during the 2016 spring semester, while 12 percent did not purchase textbooks. Of that 88 percent, the average amount of dollars spent on textbooks was $465.90 during spring 2016; however, it must be noted that many students spent far more. One student reported spending about $2,500 on textbooks for one semester, while eight students spent over $1,000. The ninety-seven survey respondents spent a total of $39,067.50 on textbooks during the spring 2016 semester. While these figures are student approximations, they illustrate underlying student concerns about overspending on textbooks.

Through five focus groups, the researchers met with fifteen students, who represent a balance of first- through fifth-year students at SUNY Canton. All focus group participants were traditional college-age students and represent the following majors from each of SUNY Canton's three academic schools: legal studies, criminal investigations, health and fitness promotion, homeland security, nursing, psychology, graphic and multimedia design, veterinary science technology, and funeral services.

It is evident that the typical student at SUNY Canton cannot afford to spend close to $500 or more on textbooks for one fifteen-week semester. Focus group participants used words such as "outrageous" and "ridiculous" when describing textbook prices, while one survey respondent noted: "Being that I pay thousands of dollars to take classes at this school, I see no reason why I should have to pay an additional $250 on a textbook that will only be applicable for the duration of the class." In fact, every survey and focus group respondent expressed dissatisfaction with textbook prices.

Already frustrated with textbooks they cannot afford, students are especially discontented when textbooks are not utilized in the course. A recurrent theme in focus group discussions was frustration over purchasing expensive texts that are rarely or never used. A majority of focus group respondents stated that they regretted purchasing a particular textbook in their college career. A junior at SUNY Canton noted that she regretted purchasing a $350 book that was never used. The student sold the book back for $100, noting that the book was "worthless to me." Other students agreed, expressing frustration over a book for an introductory course in the sciences. These students explained that the text was barely used in class and that they were only assigned to read one or two chapters throughout the semester.

When faced with overwhelming textbook prices and the risk that textbooks may not be utilized in class, many respondents decided not to purchase books at all. According to survey results, 79 percent of the respondents reported that there have been instances when the decision was made not to buy or rent expensive textbooks assigned for class. Seventy-four percent of the surveyed students were concerned that the decision could hurt their grades but made the decision based on excessive textbook costs.

Focus group respondents noted similar sentiments. One student described his own experience with failure: "There were two books that I never got for that class, and I failed." When asked if having the textbooks would have helped his grade, the student replied, "probably." A senior in funeral services administration stated, "I'm a good student, but the lower grades that I have are definitely the classes I didn't get the textbook for." In a follow-up question about why they did not purchase books, students universally cited money as the determining factor.

The potential for retention issues thrives when students are unhappy about the disuse and misuse of assigned textbooks, or when they feel overwhelmed about their inability to pay for the textbooks they need. It is evident that survey and focus group respondents believe the textbook program at SLLC is making an attempt to lift some of the financial burden from struggling students. About 52 percent of the surveyed students use the textbook reserves at SLLC, and all focus group respondents noted that they had used the reserve collection at some point in their studies. One surveyed student noted: "I could not afford to buy many of the textbooks for my program . . . Having access to the textbooks [at the library] was SO IMPORTANT."

Students additionally make a connection between the textbook reserve program and their success in the classroom. Fifty-two percent of students stated that they significantly felt having textbooks in the library had a positive impact on their academic success. Furthermore, multiple variations of the following statement came up time and again in open-ended survey responses: "I am so grateful for the textbook reserves. Without this resource I would not be able to pass my classes." Another student noted, "I have been able to excel in all of my online courses with the help of the textbooks." Furthermore, students felt reserve textbooks increased diligence in their studies. Comments such as "[reserve textbooks] motivated me to go to the library and actually sit down and get the work done since I couldn't take [the book] with me," and "[the reserve program] makes me stay out of my dorm to complete my work" additionally express this idea. Focus group participants noted the same sentiment. One student explained that "using the textbooks in the library makes me do my work . . . so I can just be free on the weekends." Not only has the textbook program contributed to academic success, but it has helped to instill a productive sense of time management among SUNY Canton students.

Not all students are using the textbook program at SLLC. About 48 percent of survey respondents noted that they do not use the textbook reserves. These students may not use the reserves for a number of reasons. Some may not be satisfied with the current collection. A few of the survey and focus group respondents noted that the library did not have the textbooks they needed, or that the library only owned old editions of their texts. Others said that the library did not own enough copies of their assigned textbooks, and that every time they visited, the book was already checked out. Additionally, other students may never use the textbook reserves because they are not aware the program exists. While the librarians at SLLC have made efforts to market the program since its inception, more must be done to increase student awareness of this service.

CONCLUSION

The importance of the SLLC textbook program to SUNY Canton students is apparent. Students believe the collection contributes to their academic success, and the results of the study support the sustainability of the program. Many students would like to see the program expanded. As SLLC librarians move forward with the textbook project, they would like to have a copy of every textbook available, which echoes student feedback such as "The library should have at least one current edition text for every class taught on this campus or online." SUNY Canton librarians recognize the program's sustainability challenge, as well as the arguments made in the literature against textbook collections. The purchased textbooks are indeed expensive, new editions are published frequently, and the collection requires labor and time for both cataloging and circulation. Despite these obstacles, SLLC is committed to its user-centered textbook initiative. SLLC is confident this project will have a significant impact on student well-being and success, and therefore a positive effect on student retention. As a result of this study, and in an effort to remain outward-facing and committed to enhanced user experiences, SLLC has established the following goal for the 2016–17 academic year: the acquisition of as many 100-level course textbooks as possible.

SLLC also hopes to grow the textbook program through the addition of open educational resources, and is confident that this initiative would be positively accepted by SUNY Canton students. Eighty-one percent of student survey respondents would prefer for their professors to change existing course-related readings to a free and open electronic textbook, and 66 percent felt that using a free electronic textbook would have a positive impact on their grade in a course.[15] As OERs gain credibility and popularity among academics, textbook programs will have an increased financial ability to meet student needs.

Survey and focus group respondents also suggested the need for increased campus support of the textbook program. For instance, one survey respondent noted: "The school should always provide the option to supply textbooks in the library so that students don't fear failing classes because they cannot afford the books the teachers require." SLLC is committed to maintaining and improving this student-centered initiative, and will advocate for increased buy-in among administrative and faculty stakeholders. The results of this study will be distributed campus-wide, and the dean of academic support services will advocate the importance of this program as a retention effort. Additional funding from administrators has already been secured for the coming academic year, a testament to the perceived value and sustainability of the program.

Acquiring and maintaining a robust textbook collection, especially one supplemented with OERs and supported by campus administrators, can contribute to student satisfaction and academic success. The program at SLLC may serve as a model for other institutions hoping to implement a textbook collection. The authors hope libraries that adopt this practice have the opportunity to directly contribute to campus retention efforts, a meaningful measure of an academic library's value.

Notes

1. Consumer Price Index, Bureau of Labor Statistics, www.bls.gov/cpi/.
2. Brice Austin, *Reserves, Electronic Reserves, and Copyright: The Past and the Future* (Philadelphia: Haworth Information, 2004).
3. John H. Pollitz, Anne Christie, and Cheryl Middleton, "Management of Library Course Reserves and the Textbook Affordability Crisis," *Journal of Access Services* 6 (2009).

4. Cynthia Hsieh and Rhonelle Runner, "Textbooks, Leisure Reading, and the Academic Library," *Library Collections, Acquisitions, & Technical Services* 29, no. 3-4 (2005).

5. John H. Pollitz and Anne Christie, "The High Cost of Textbooks: A Convergence of Academic Libraries, Campus Bookstores, and Publishers?" *Electronic Journal of Academic and Special Librarianship* 7 (Summer 2006); Laura Kane McElfresh, "College Textbooks and Libraries: If You Reserve It, They Will Come," *Technicalities* 29 (November/December 2009).

6. Bonnie Imler, "Troublesome Textbooks: Students Confuse the Roles of the Library and the Bookstore," *American Libraries* (November 2009).

7. Donald A. Barclay, "No Reservations: Why the Time Has Come to Kill Print Textbook Reserves," *College & Research Libraries News* 76, no. 6 (2015): 333, http://crln.acrl.org/content/76/6/332.full.

8. Steven Bell, "Occupy Textbooks: Drop Out and Try Something New," *From the Bell Tower* (blog), December 8, 2011, http://lj.libraryjournal.com/2011/12/opinion/steven-bell/occupy-textbooks-drop-out-and-try-something-new-from-the-bell-tower/; Joe Moxley, "Who Is Best Suited to Control Textbooks: The Faculty or the Publishers? There Are Ways to Make Sure It Is the Faculty," *AAUP Open Textbook Publishing,* September-October 2013, https://www.aaup.org/article/open-textbook-publishing; Steven Bell, "Openness to Textbook Alternatives Is Growing," *From the Bell Tower,* October 2, 2013, http://lj.libraryjournal.com/2013/10/opinion/steven-bell/openness-to-textbooks-alternatives-is-growing from-the-bell-tower/; Steven Bell, "Five Institutional Strategies for Textbook Affordability," *From the Bell Tower,* February 4, 2016, http://lj.libraryjournal.com/2016/02/opinion/steven-bell/five-institutional-strategies-for textbook-affordability-from-the-bell-tower/; and many others.

9. Julie Middlemas, Patricia Morrison, and Nadra Farina-Hess, "Reserve Textbooks: To Buy, or Not to Buy?" *Library Philosophy & Practice* (2012), http://digitalcommons.unl.edu/libphilprac/796/; Caroline Crouse, "Textbooks 101: Textbook Collection at the University of Minnesota," *Journal of Access Services* 5, no. 1-2 (2007), http://dx.doi.org/10.1080/15367960802199026.

10. Crouse, "Textbooks 101," 285.

11. Krista McDonald and John Burke, "The Case for Textbooks: Our Service Traditions Call for Us to Provide Them," *American Libraries* (March 2010).

12. Ibid, 25.

13. Middlemas, Morrison, and Farina-Hess, "Reserve Textbooks," 8.

14. Jeremy Sayles, "The Textbooks-in-College-Libraries Mystery," *College & Undergraduate Libraries* 1 (1994): 87, http://dx.doi.org/10.1300/J106v01n01_10.

15. Another survey respondent wrote the following quote, which serves as an important commentary on a very real issue that may arise as the result of the textbook affordability crisis on the SUNY Canton campus: "I strongly believe that each professor should

have one copy of their texts either physically in the library or electronically through our e-library. If they feel that it is important enough for us to purchase, they should have a copy for those who can't. It might prove an unfair academic advantage for some students over others. There should not be an academic gap simply because some students have to decide between having enough food for the semester and buying textbooks."

Bibliography

Austin, Brice. *Reserves, Electronic Reserves, and Copyright: The Past and the Future.* Philadelphia: Haworth Information, 2004.

Barclay, Donald A. "No Reservations: Why the Time Has Come to Kill Print Textbook Reserves." *College & Research Libraries News* 76, no. 6 (2015): 332–35. http://crln.acrl .org/content/76/6/332.full.

Bureau of Labor Statistics. Consumer Price Index. www.bls.gov/cpi/.

Crouse, Caroline. "Textbooks 101: Textbook Collection at the University of Minnesota." *Journal of Access Services* 5, no. 1-2 (2007): 285–93. http://dx.doi.org/10.1080/ 15367960802199026.

Hsieh, Cynthia, and Rhonelle Runner. "Textbooks, Leisure Reading, and the Academic Library." *Library Collections, Acquisitions, & Technical Services* 29, no. 2 (2005): 192–204. http://dx.doi.org/10.1016/j.lcats.2005.04.005.

Imler, Bonnie. "Troublesome Textbooks: Students Confuse the Roles of the Library and the Bookstore." *American Libraries* (November 2009): 35.

McDonald, Krista, and John Burke. "The Case for Textbooks: Our Service Traditions Call for Us to Provide Them." *American Libraries* (March 2010): 25.

McElfresh, Laura Kane. "College Textbooks and Libraries: If You Reserve It, They Will Come." *Technicalities* 29 (November/December 2009): 4–6.

Middlemas, Julie, Patricia Morrison, and Nadra Farina-Hess. "Reserve Textbooks: To Buy, or Not to Buy?" *Library Philosophy & Practice* (2012): 1–9. http://digitalcommons.unl.edu/ libphilprac/796/.

Pollitz, John H., and Anne Christie. "The High Cost of Textbooks: A Convergence of Academic Libraries, Campus Bookstores, and Publishers?" *Electronic Journal of Academic and Special Librarianship* 7, no. 2 (2006), http://hdl.handle.net/1957/3011.

Pollitz, John H., Anne Christie, and Cheryl Middleton. "Management of Library Course and the Textbook Affordability Crisis." *Journal of Access Services* 6, no. 4 (2009): 459–84, doi: 10.1080/15367960903149268.

Sayles, Jeremy. "The Textbooks-in-College-Libraries Mystery." *College & Undergraduate Libraries* 1 (1994): 81–92. http://dx.doi.org/10.1300/J106v01n01_10.

ACCESS AND AFFORDABILITY
The Textbook Conundrum

Peggy Seiden and Amy McColl

This chapter is the story of how the Swarthmore College Libraries conceived of and implemented a program that, at the time, flew in the face of standard academic collection development principles, as well as many faculty members' wishes. In response to student concerns, the libraries have purchased all assigned textbooks and placed them on reserve in their libraries for the past six years. The program has evolved over time in several directions. We have integrated the program with our e-book collection strategy, and this past year we implemented a textbook exchange/clearinghouse so that students could donate the past year's textbooks for other students to use, rather than selling them back to the bookstore. We are also hosting workshops to educate students on legal alternatives to purchasing their textbooks.

Swarthmore College (Swarthmore, Pennsylvania) is home to slightly over 1,500 undergraduates and 211 faculty. It is nearly unique among liberal arts colleges in that it has a general engineering program in addition to programs in the arts, humanities, social sciences, and sciences. It has a fairly open curriculum with minimal requirements: students take three courses in each of the major divisions (humanities, social sciences, and sciences), though advanced placement credits can go towards meeting these. There is also a requirement to take three writing-intensive courses and at least twenty courses outside of one's major. Swarthmore College has a main library, McCabe, and two branch libraries: the Cornell Library for Science and Engineering and the Daniel C. Underhill Library for the Performing Arts. The McCabe, Cornell, and Daniel C. Underhill libraries house their own reserves collections appropriate to the disciplines supported therein.

As a community, Swarthmore has become increasingly concerned with the affordability of a college education. Swarthmore's core values derive from its Quaker beginnings. In our most recent strategic planning process, community members identified these values as respect for the individual, consensus decision-making, simple living, social responsibility and justice, generous giving, and the peaceful settlement of disputes. These values in turn underpin one of our key strengths: our desire to provide access and opportunity for all students, regardless of their financial circumstances.[1]

Swarthmore is one of a decreasing minority of institutions that continue a policy of "need blind" admissions and who meet the full demonstrated need of all admitted students. Need blind admissions refers to the college's policy to accept students only on merit, without considering their ability to pay their fees. In 2007 the college instituted a no loan policy, in which all financial aid from the college is in the form of grants or work-study. Fifty-three percent of our students are on financial aid, with the average aid award at about $45,800 out of $61,400 in total fees, excluding educational materials and personal expenses. Estimated expenses for books are about $1,350.[2] The number of first-year students who qualify for aid continues to increase and is now just under 58 percent.[3]

OUR HISTORICAL RESERVE PROGRAM

The focus on using reserves to provide students with access to textbooks fits well within the traditional library practices of the college. Swarthmore has always had a robust course reserves program. There are both general reserve and honors reserve in all three of its libraries. The "honors reserve" is an open collection arranged by honors seminars. The earliest mention of the "reserves shelf" in the library dates back to 1915, though in all probability it existed long before that date.[4] Faculty routinely assigned significant amounts of reading beyond that in required textbooks. In addition to monographs, faculty or their administrative assistants put together binders of readings on reserve, rather than selling course packs in the bookstore. With the advent of the electronic reserves program, these binders have all but disappeared. For years, students would line up before 9 p.m. in front of the main circulation/reserves desk to check materials out overnight. Faculty in the sciences also place personal copies of texts on reserve so that students can consult them as needed without having to carry the books around with them all day.

While there is no definitive evidence to support the following, it seems that the primacy of the reserves program as a core piece of the academic program may be linked to the college's honors program developed in 1920–21. Frank Aydelotte, then president of the college, proposed a program based upon the Oxford model in which "attendance at lectures and classes should be entirely voluntary, and . . . the honors degree should depend upon the student's success in a series of examinations."[5] Students would prepare for these tests through their *independent reading* and through instruction offered by the college; the central idea was for students to take greater responsibility for their intellectual growth rather than to "spoon-feed" them.[6] As the program took shape, so too did the idea that students would master a body of literature associated with a particular honors seminar or topic. The amount of reading was not prescribed, though students were expected to do background reading for each seminar meeting. A period of significant growth of the library's collection coincided directly with the initiation of the honors program. In *An Adventure in Education,* a 1941 treatise on the honors program by an anonymous group of Swarthmore faculty, the authors write: "reading for honors brings a higher percentage of its votaries to the library's resources and keeps man and book together for longer periods than is the case under any less exacting course of study." The honors reserves collection was also noted to be both broader and more scholarly than that of typical undergraduate institutions.[7] Reading lists included "few if any college textbooks" but focused instead on original documents and classics, and only then should students "consult commentaries, criticisms, and textbook renderings."[8] Charles B. Shaw, librarian of the college during the establishment and rapid growth of the honors program, introduced many modern library practices in his first decade and garnered significantly greater support for both materials and staffing.[9] Today the honors reserves collection is comprised of nearly 8,000 items in support of 123 seminars.

HISTORY OF SWARTHMORE'S TEXTBOOK PURCHASING PROGRAM

Concerns about the cost of textbooks and reliance on the library's reserve shelf as a solution are not new. A 1962 article in *The Phoenix*, Swarthmore College's student newspaper, noted so, as seen in this excerpt:[10]

> AS EVERY good student knows, the purchase of text-books has become in recent years a major financial burden. With the price of even paperbacks spiraling, students have put more pressure on the rather limited reserves of the library, while some professors have been forced to abandon the "right" books for some less worthy but cheaper texts. Yet even these undesirable, "last-ditch" solutions have proved inadequate; the average Swarthmore student finds book-purchases accounting for an increasingly higher proportion of his total school expenditures.

For many years, Access and Lending staff solicited textbook information from faculty members each semester, and professors and instructors would send annotated lists back to the library, including the call number if the library already owned the book. Orders were then placed for titles not already held in the libraries' collections. This system was not comprehensive, and it relied on faculty members' response and getting the information in time to have the books placed on reserve before the start of classes, but it was largely successful in getting the majority of required readings on the reserve shelf. In more recent years as faculty retired and new faculty members were hired, this system was not quite as effective, and we found that the bookstore was getting more comprehensive required textbook lists from the faculty. We considered ways in which the library could work with the bookstore to streamline the ordering process.

Following the economic downturn that began in 2008, Swarthmore Student Council members began discussions with administrators at the college to bring attention to the fact that some students, including students on full scholarships, were not able to afford to buy all of their required textbooks. These concerns were discussed in an article appearing in the student-edited online journal *The Daily Gazette* in October 2008. Author Allie Lee stated, "Textbook prices have long been a hot issue among college students and their parents. Even though $200-$500 for books per semester is not that much in comparison to tuition costs at most private colleges, buying books is yet another source of financial stress."[11]

At the beginning of the 2009–10 academic year, new Student Council members stated that not enough research had been done to find the most efficient way to resolve the problem of high textbook costs, and a campus forum was planned for November 16, 2009, in order to bring together key players. A description of the forum that appeared in the student newspaper *The Phoenix* read as follows: "Class Awareness Month and Student Council will host a discussion about textbook buying. The event aims to bring students, faculty, staff and librarians together to help alleviate the burdening costs of textbooks and educate students about how the system works. This will give students a chance to voice their thoughts while also hearing why some options simply won't work. One goal is to better explain why the textbook system currently works the way it does and what can be done to improve it."[12]

Student turnout at the forum was very low, fewer than a dozen students, according to a *Phoenix* article published November 19, 2009, but the discussion was lively. The student financial policy representative, Dan Symonds, stated: "We wanted to make people aware that [the Student Council]'s concerned about textbooks and we wanted to solicit as many ideas as possible."[13] Former bookstore director Kathy Grace pointed out that the store actually lost money on selling textbooks:

> Grace explained that the college bookstore is already losing money on textbooks because it raises the textbook price by 20 percent on top of the net price instead of the 25 percent industry standard. While the bookstore is expected to make money, she says that the money is made from sweatshirts and other merchandise, not textbooks. "About three years ago we started losing money on textbooks," Grace said. "A lot of students would buy the books or order the books online, and then return the books, so we're paying all the merchant fees on nothing, and those add up." Grace also points out that a major problem for the bookstore is that many faculty members do not provide information about required books for their classes until the winter or summer break, making it difficult for the bookstore to find used copies to sell the next year. "If we know the faculty will use a book the next semester, then we can put a guaranteed buyback sticker on it and the student can buy the book at 75 [percent] and sell it at 50, so they're only spending 25 on a textbook, which is a pretty good deal," Grace said.[14]

Her comment about the timeliness of getting book lists from faculty members points to another development in 2008, the passing of the Higher Education Opportunities Act (HEOA) into law, which included a textbook provision that went into effect July 2010, which requires college bookstores to make bibliographic, pricing, purchase, and rental information available to students.[15]

In order for bookstores to make this information available early enough for students to have choices in terms of textbook purchase or rental, the book lists must be finalized by faculty members in a timely fashion, which is a challenge for all. Also from the same *Phoenix* article:

> Biology professor Scott Gilbert said that many new textbooks are sent by publishers late in the semester, preventing the professors from choosing new books until later. Gilbert has written three textbooks himself. "The reason why textbooks are so expensive is because after the first semester, the used book market kicks in and the publisher, the artist and the writer get nothing," Gilbert said.[16]

At the forum, the director of financial aid, Laura Talbot, stated that in 2008–09 the college spent $870,000 in textbook allowances for students.[17] However, there is no way to ensure that the money awarded as part of the aid package for books is actually spent on textbooks. Following the forum, library staff met and decided that the fairest way to spend the grant money would be to try to purchase required textbooks which were not already owned by the libraries and place them on the reserve shelves. While not a perfect solution, the plan would allow students equitable access to free copies of their required readings.

WHAT DO WE MEAN BY TEXTBOOKS?

When we proposed trying to address textbook affordability by purchasing all of the textbooks assigned by faculty, there was a certain amount of resistance among staff. The chief concern was that the project would eat into our general monographs budget and that many standard textbooks would need yearly updating. However, given that 80 percent of monographs that are purchased "just in case" are used only 20 percent of the time, it seemed that directing our funds to purchasing materials that would be in demand was more than a good investment; it was a social good. We also recognized that only a small percentage of courses—typically introductory courses in biology, chemistry, economics, psychology, and foreign languages—required students to purchase standard textbooks, although the difference between a "textbook" and other scholarly works is often blurry at best. Is a standard edition of Sophocles that is used in an introductory drama course a textbook? What about the *Norton Anthology of Poetry?* Even with a very liberal definition of "textbook," only 5 percent of the purchases in the last two years were scholarly works.

As we reviewed the lists of required textbooks, we soon discovered that the vast majority of materials aligned with our general collection development policy and that the lists served as an excellent collection development tool. In the past, much of the general collection had been built from faculty requests, but as we moved to a slip approval program and faculty workload increased, fewer and fewer faculty took responsibility for ensuring that collections in their fields were up-to-date. Materials selection fell on the shoulders of the research and instruction librarians with little input from faculty. We were unaware that certain editions of literary, philosophical, or religious texts that were in our collection were not necessarily the ones that faculty were using with their classes. A side benefit of the project was reconnecting with the faculty and curriculum, albeit not in as direct a manner as when faculty drove much of the materials acquisition.

Students were not simply distressed about purchasing a $200 textbook; they were concerned about the number of scholarly monographs and editions of texts required for literature, classics, history, philosophy, and religion courses which could easily add up to more than $200 per course. As a point of reference, in one semester surveyed, the average cost for students to buy required texts for a single course over all disciplines was $151. The most expensive course for that semester, a political science class, had a total textbook price tag of $466. Furthermore, faculty rarely asked students to read critical and scholarly works in their entirety. It was more likely that they would assign several chapters over the course of a semester. A reserve collection would allow students to make personal photocopies of chapters in the same way they once did for journal articles.

INITIATION OF THE TEXTBOOK PURCHASING PROGRAM IN THE LIBRARIES

At the end of the 2008–09 academic year, the Swarthmore College Student Council found that it had a surplus of rollover funds, and members suggested that the organization could spend a portion of that money to alleviate the financial burdens of students who could not afford to buy all of their books. A decision was made to donate $10,000 of the rollover money to the library, but no consensus was reached on how best to spend the funds. Some ideas included purchasing textbooks for the library reserve collection, starting a textbook rental program, creating a textbook donation program on campus, buying a print-on-demand station, and purchasing e-textbook licenses which could serve a greater number of students. In the end, it was decided that using the funds to buy required textbooks for the library collection would have the most immediate positive impact.

Starting in the spring semester of 2010, the libraries began to spend the $10,000 received from the Student Council on texts designated as required readings by faculty members. Initially, the textbook coordinator for the bookstore sent a list of courses along with required text information, including ISBN and abbreviated titles, to Acquisitions staff, who then searched the catalog to see if the library already owned the title. If so, the call number information was added to the title information and sent to an Access and Lending Staff member, who placed the book on reserve. If the title or edition was not owned by the library, Acquisitions staff placed an order for the book, and when received, the title was placed directly on reserve for that class. Over time, the bookstore changed its presentation of required textbook information to comply with HEOA, offering lists of courses along with required textbooks and the various options for acquiring the readings, including links to rental sites, used copies from various sites, and new copies from either the bookstore or from Amazon.com. The library staff used the revised website to print out lists of textbooks for each course, and annotated the lists for Access and Lending staff with relevant information. The process continues to evolve, and bookstore and library staff now use a single shared spreadsheet in order to disseminate textbook information as quickly as possible.

Surprisingly, the $10,000 allocated for textbook purchases in spring 2010 lasted into the 2012 spring semester. Due to the previous practice of collecting solicited textbook lists from faculty members, the library already owned a good percentage of the textbooks on the lists, and that minimized the expenses. When the Student Council funds ran out, the college librarian, Peggy Seiden, agreed to continue the program using library budget dollars from our monographs budget line, and we have continued to purchase required texts as needed. Of course, the program is not perfect: the bookstore lists are generated by information sent by faculty members, and if no information is received for a particular course, the library cannot purchase the books. Some faculty members never send their lists to the bookstore, preferring instead to provide course materials that they have authored and/or compiled directly to students via Moodle, the course management system, or their own websites. Some faculty members continue the practice of sending annotated lists directly to the Access and Lending Department. Additionally, unless the bookstore receives explicit information from the professor about which edition, translator, ISBN, or publisher will be used, the edition which is readily available in bulk will be chosen and ordered for sale in the store. Despite these challenges, over the past six years we have built an extensive collection of textbooks and required readings that is available free of charge to our students through our reserves program. An additional bonus is that this practice has allowed us to update our teaching collection to reflect the latest editions and newest translations of core textbooks, which might not otherwise have been added to the collection.

E-BOOK COLLECTIONS AND TEXTBOOK RESERVES

In 2011 the TriColleges (Swarthmore, Bryn Mawr, and Haverford Libraries) began a demand-driven acquisition (DDA) program with EBL, which is now a part of ProQuest e-books, and e-books became a more significant piece of our overall collection strategy. We are also subscribers to ebrary's Academic Complete collection of e-book titles, the eDuke Books Scholarly Collection, and the ACLS Humanities E-Book package. In 2015 we participated in a JSTOR Books DDA program via our state consortium, the Pennsylvania Academic Library Consortium, Inc. (PALCI), which will continue this year with some changes (backlist titles will be via PALCI in an EBA program; front list titles will be available via DDA through a TriColleges deal). In 2016 we joined the Project MUSE UPCC evidence-based program via Lyrasis, so access to e-book packages has continued to grow.

In order to provide more access to required textbooks, we link the e-book records in our OPAC to our course reserves system (see figure 2.1), giving students another way to access course content.

We continue to buy print copies of all required textbooks, so the e-books linked from these packages offer supplemental access. The downside of most of these e-book interfaces (with the exception of JSTOR and MUSE) is the digital rights management (DRM) limitation placed on printing and downloading by individual publishers, which can be frustrating for our patrons. As a result of DRM restrictions, along with evidence that our students still prefer to read monographs in print, we always buy a copy of the print book for the reserve shelf, even if the e-book version is available in our catalog.

As different models become available, we have on occasion bought single-title licenses for e-book content, but library licenses are difficult to come by and terms can be unnecessarily complex in the textbook publishing arena. Most of the single e-book titles we have bought for reserves have been large

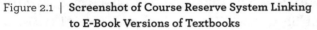

tripod

Classic Login

RESEARCH GUIDES | OTHER COLLECTIONS | BORROWING BEYOND TRI-CO | OFF CAMPUS ACCESS | SERVICES

classic

● Start Over

COURSE ▼ | engl 114 | Search

◀ Previous Record | Next Record ▶

Profita Cohen, L
Course ENGL 114 Swarthmore
English 114 Swarthmore
Early American Media Cultures Swarthmore
Cour note Fall 2015

RESERVES LIST			
Title	Author	Call #	Format
Always already new : media, history and the data of culture / Lisa Gitelman	Gitelman, Lisa	Swarthmore: McCabe Honors 4 weeks -- ENGL 114 Swarthmore -- AVAILABLE	
Always already new [electronic resource] : media, history and the data of culture / Lisa Gitelman.	Gitelman, Lisa.	Swarthmore: Web Access -- -- ONLINE	
The amalgamation waltz [electronic resource] : race, performance, and the ruses of memory / Tavia Nyo	Ochieng' Nyongó, Tavia Amolo	Swarthmore: Web Access -- E184.A1 O25 2009eb -- ONLINE	
American archives : gender, race, and class in visual culture / Shawn Michelle Smith	Smith, Shawn Michelle, 1965-	Swarthmore: McCabe Honors 4 weeks -- ENGL 114 Swarthmore -- AVAILABLE	
American literature and the culture of reprinting, 1834-1853 / Meredith L. McGill	McGill, Meredith L	Swarthmore: McCabe Honors 4 weeks -- ENGL 114 Swarthmore -- AVAILABLE	
American literature and the culture of reprinting, 1834-1853 [electronic resource] / Meredith L. McGi	McGill, Meredith L	Swarthmore: Web Access -- Z479 .M34 2007eb -- ONLINE	
The business of letters : authorial economies in antebellum America / Leon Jackson	Jackson, Leon, 1965-	Swarthmore: McCabe Honors 4 weeks -- ENGL 114 Swarthmore -- AVAILABLE	
The camera and the press : American visual and print culture in the age of the daguerreotype / Marcy	Dinius, Marcy J	Swarthmore: McCabe Honors 4 weeks -- ENGL 114 Swarthmore -- AVAILABLE	
City reading : written words and public spaces in antebellum New York / David M. Henkin	Henkin, David M	Swarthmore: McCabe Honors 4 weeks -- ENGL 114 Swarthmore c.2 -- AVAILABLE	
The common pot : the recovery of native space in the Northeast / Lisa Brooks	Brooks, Lisa Tanya	Swarthmore: McCabe Honors 4 weeks -- ENGL 114 Swarthmore -- AVAILABLE	

Figure 2.1 | **Screenshot of Course Reserve System Linking to E-Book Versions of Textbooks**

reference works, as well as some scholarly monographs purchased via EBL or ebrary on a bibliographer's or faculty member's recommendation. However, with data from a 2014 survey of our students' habits with regard to textbooks revealing that 40.7 percent would prefer to use print textbooks and only 4.1 percent would prefer to use e-books, we are likely to continue to prefer print and only purchase e-book content when specifically requested.[18]

STUDENT STRATEGIES FOR GETTING TEXTBOOKS

The college last participated in the National Association of College Stores Student Watch survey during fall 2014. The association administers the survey each semester to determine student purchasing patterns for course materials. The Swarthmore College bookstore issued an open invitation to participate in the survey to all students and slightly over 11 percent (172 students) answered the survey. Thirty-six percent of the respondents were first-year students; 18 percent were sophomores; 24 percent were juniors; and 21 percent were seniors. While the low return rate does not permit a high level of confidence in the findings, it does provide some sense of student textbook access patterns, and where national data was available, the findings align with those data. While 88 percent of first-year students purchased their course materials, only 77 percent of seniors purchased any of their books. The number of students who borrowed materials increased from 14.5 percent (first-years) to 37 percent (seniors). The number of students who said they acquired textbooks though Internet download/piracy rose from 13 percent (first-years) to 26 percent (seniors). When asked what their main reason was for not acquiring course materials, 54 percent answered that they could get the materials elsewhere without purchase, though another 46 percent answered that they didn't want or need them.[19]

As part of the research for this chapter, we also interviewed ten undergraduates who represented all class years and majors in all three divisions as well as two recent alumna. While not all of their behaviors aligned with the findings of the survey, these conversations did help to flesh out the general data. Even among confessed bibliophiles—students who routinely spend hours in used bookstores and spend discretionary funds on building their own book collections—few of the students interviewed about their textbook acquisition habits purchase all the required materials for their courses. While some students prefer to purchase materials for their major areas of study and find other means of getting materials for courses that fulfill divisional requirements, others purchase only those materials that have personal meaning or value, such as poetry or fiction, and find other ways of procuring their remaining textbooks. Some use reserves, while others search for e-books in the catalog, JSTOR, or Google.com. These students are creative, innovative and collaborative, sharing their strategies for procuring texts or the actual textbooks.

A student will employ a variety of strategies depending on how she values the content and whether it will be useful to her in the future. The student might purchase a used textbook even if it is an older version, particularly if it will be used in more than one course; she might rent another textbook through Amazon.com; if the course requires a series of paperbacks, she might look for used copies or rent them through the bookstore or look for assigned materials online in the learning management system or through the library. Several students who study languages indicated that they would purchase dictionaries, because they will use them over their entire academic careers. Furthermore, the textbook habits of students evolve over the course of their four years. Frequently, first-year students will purchase most if not all of their textbooks, but by their junior year, they have developed other means of securing access to the textbook content.

While students use the textbooks in the reserve collection, they often want or need to keep the materials for longer periods of time than the allotted two hours. If they only require a chapter or two, they may scan the necessary pages, though others may take notes. Another strategy is to try and secure the materials through interlibrary loan or borrow the books from within our consortium from Bryn Mawr or Haverford. The PALCI EZBorrow system (a disintermediated system used by over fifty libraries in Pennsylvania and surrounding states) allows for semester-long borrowing and materials cannot be recalled.

The majority of students prefer to have their own copies of materials, and though some are content with digital copies, many still prefer print that they can mark up. Preference for print remains strong according to a recent national survey from the National Association of College Stores, which confirms findings from a reading preferences survey that Swarthmore conducted during spring 2015.[20]

Sixty-nine percent of the students responding to the fall 2014 NACS survey purchased materials from the college store, while 62 percent said they purchased materials from Amazon. In the interviews, students said they use Amazon.com to seek out used copies if those are significantly less expensive. However, 80 percent of our local NACS survey respondents noted that all things being equal, they would prefer to purchase or rent their materials from the college bookstore.[21]

Several students confessed to strategies that are distinctly unethical, if not illegal. These strategies included

- Purchasing international editions of textbooks which are usually significantly cheaper than the U.S. editions
- Using online discussion forums, such as Internet Relay Chat clients, as a means of finding exact editions of textbooks that have been scanned and are available as PDFs by students all over the world
- Purchasing textbooks, scanning them, and sharing the PDFs with classmates over the local file-sharing system, and returning the textbook for a refund

For students who grew up post-Napster, the perception is that file sharing raises few, if any ethical issues.

THE FACULTY PERSPECTIVE

Faculty are by now well aware of the additional financial burden of textbooks and do not always demand that students have the most recent edition of a textbook. However, many faculty still feel that for students to fully grasp the course material they need to purchase the textbooks. As one faculty member wrote:

> Having a book means (whether realistically or not) "ownership" of the course or the material. Like other things, I think that if a person makes an investment (literally) into a course by actually paying money to get the book, they will feel the responsibility of allocating more time for the course.[22]

This belief is held by many faculty, but seems particularly true for faculty in the foreign languages and economics. It's unclear whether faculty are fully aware of the extent to which students have developed other strategies for accessing the content.

Scott Gilbert, an emeritus faculty member, who has authored the seminal textbook in developmental biology, noted that introductory texts do not necessarily need to be revised as often as advanced texts which need to convey the state of the art. He revises his own textbook every three years and estimates that one-third of the content is new. Just as it is likely that faculty are not fully aware of how students acquire course materials, he writes that he thinks most students are unaware of what goes into the writing and production of textbooks.[23]

A few faculty have tried to address the high cost of textbooks by putting together their own course text and making it freely available to their students. We know of only one case where a department tried to use an open textbook, in this case for the first year biology course. This "experiment" was deemed to be a failure, noting that the introductory biology text from OpenStax was incomplete and sections were missing or poorly written.

In some disciplines, faculty make most of the course readings available via the Moodle learning management system. In essence, these readings are similar to course packs, but where possible, the Moodle system directly links to the publisher's PDF.

ASSESSING THE SUCCESS OF THE TEXTBOOK PURCHASING PROGRAM

The students who were interviewed were asked specifically about their use of reserves to access textbooks. While students were aware that the libraries had all course textbooks on reserve, and they all were selective when it came to purchasing textbooks, their use of these materials was highly individualistic. Those that used reserves, used them heavily and the others didn't use them at all. One student remarked that the quality of the scanner in the science library precluded her use. Others complained about a loan period of only two hours.

We have begun to do in-depth analysis of the use of the reserve textbook program. This fall we analyzed 200 courses (approximately half of the courses offered that semester in order to get a minimal error rate of 5 percent). Of these, 125 courses had at least one required textbook. (Note: We placed any and all required textbooks on reserve.) For each course we looked at the number and cost of all required texts, the number of unique items and total copies on reserve, enrollment, and circulation of the two most expensive books. We have not yet completed a full statistical analysis, but we have observed certain patterns in the data.

Circulation patterns are distinctly different for the sciences and the humanities/ social sciences. On average, the science courses have two required textbooks on reserve, while courses in the humanities or social sciences average just under seven. Each textbook in the sciences circulated an average of 27.6 times over the semester; in the humanities/social sciences that number was only 2.8 times. Many of the required items in the humanities and social sciences never circulated.

In order to try and identify why some items circulate and others do not, we are also analyzing pricing data. We are examining whether the most expensive required books also have the highest circulation rates, but thus far we do not see any patterns emerging. It is likely that for courses in the humanities and social sciences, some other factors drive circulation. One other pattern of note: where a discipline has a defined series of graduated courses (mostly in the sciences), circulation rates for upper-level courses are higher than for lower-level courses. This finding would seem to align with the NACS data and our interviews wherein upper-level students acknowledged buying fewer course materials than first-year students and sophomores.

While we were initially anxious about the costs that would be incurred once the Student Council grant money ran out, we have found that our total expenditures on textbooks generally decrease each year, since faculty members tend to use the same basic textbooks for courses in following years. Of course, new and visiting faculty teach in new areas, requiring a higher outlay when a new course is first taught, but overall, costs have not been excessive. In 2014–15 total costs were $6,776, which equals about 2.5 percent of our total print monographs budget, and in 2015–16 the cost went down to $5,406, a mere 2 percent.

TEXTBOOK DONATION AND WORKSHOP PILOT PROGRAM

During the summer 2015, the Dean of Students Office approached the library about ways in which we could support first-generation students. Our performing arts librarian, Donna Fournier, herself a first-generation college student, volunteered to work with the dean of first-year students on helping these students and other low-income students secure textbooks. They developed a two-pronged approach:

1. The development of a textbook collection through donations
2. An educational program including workshops and a LibGuide to help students understand the options available to them beyond the purchase of textbooks

The initial call for donations at the end of the fall and spring terms through posters and e-mail resulted in only a shelf's worth of books each time. Enter Trash to Treasures—an annual fund-raising effort that resells materials students have donated or left behind at the end of the spring semester. We were able to secure consensus from the Trash to Treasures committee that they would donate any textbooks they received or found to this collection. There were over 800 textbooks donated, of which over 500 were added to the fledgling textbook collection. Currently, these materials are housed in the Performing Arts Library and students are invited to browse and borrow what they need. The textbooks are cataloged, but the records are suppressed from public view and only students that are pre-identified by the Dean's Office are invited to use the collection. While students borrow materials for the term in which they need them, there is no penalty if they choose to keep the textbooks.

The first workshop was held in fall 2015 after students had registered for their spring courses, and a second one was held in January after students had received their syllabi. We targeted first-generation students identified through the Dean's Office. The workshops covered the pros and cons of ownership; how to locate materials to borrow; and how to search the catalog and interlibrary loan resources to identify materials. In addition, we developed a LibGuide (http://libguides.brynmawr.edu/swat-textbooks) that provides guidance on "how to borrow instead of buy." The 2016–17 academic year was the first year that students had access to the collection of donated textbooks. But it is clear that it is not only first-generation or low-income students who are looking for other ways to procure needed textbooks. Whether the collection can be opened to others is a question worth revisiting with the dean of students.

CONCLUSION

Faculty and students are concerned about the quality and the cost of textbooks. As established in the early part of the previous century, the honors program has had a continuing influence on the types and quantity of course materials that faculty assign to their students. It is unlikely that faculty patterns will change in the near future. While faculty in the large introductory courses in the sciences and social sciences may look to open educational resources to supplement course materials, it is unlikely that they will move wholesale in this direction. As the number of students on financial aid continues to increase, we will continue to educate them about their options.

Notes

1. Swarthmore College, *Strategic Directions for Swarthmore College* (Swarthmore, PA: Swarthmore College, 2011), http://sp.swarthmore.edu/wp-content/uploads/2012/01/StratPlan_Booklet_12e3.pdf.
2. Swarthmore College, "Swarthmore College Financial Aid Statistics," *College Fact Book* (Swarthmore, PA: Swarthmore College, 2016), www.swarthmore.edu/sites/default/files/assets/documents/institutional-research/FAStats.pdf.
3. Robin Shores, e-mail message to author, August 2, 2016.
4. "College Debating," *The Phoenix* 35, no. 4 (October 12, 1915): 2.
5. Frank Aydelotte. *Breaking the Academic Lock Step: The Development of Honors Work in American Colleges and Universities* (New York: Harper & Brothers, 1944), 33.
6. Ibid., 32.
7. Swarthmore College Faculty, *An Adventure in Education: Swarthmore College under Frank Aydelotte* (New York: Macmillan, 1941), 141.

8. Robert C. Brooks, *Reading for Honors at Swarthmore: A Record of the First Five Years, 1922–1927* (New York: Oxford University Press, 1927), 21.

9. Charles B. Shaw, librarian of the college from 1927 to 1962, edited the first edition of *A List of Books for College Libraries* (Chicago, 1931). Faculty from the college contributed to the selected list of books.

10. "ISCU," *The Phoenix* 82, no. 36 (March 13, 1962): 2. http://triptych.brynmawr.edu/cdm/ref/collection/SC_Phoenix/id/14854.

11. Allie Lee; "Cheaper Online Textbook Options Not Popular," *Daily Gazette* (October 7, 2008).

12. "Events Menu: Textbook Costs," *The Phoenix* 35, no. 11 (November 12, 2009): 3.

13. Linda Hou, "Forum Addresses Textbook Issues," *The Phoenix* 35, no. 12 (November 19, 2009): 3.

14. Ibid.

15. Section 133, Higher Education Opportunity Act, Pub. L. No. 110-315, 122 Stat. 3107 (August 14, 2008), https://www.gpo.gov/fdsys/pkg/PLAW-110pub1315/pdf/PLAW-110pub1315.pdf.

16. Hou, "Forum Addresses Textbook Issues," 3.

17. Ibid.

18. National Association of College Stores, "Student Watch Data Fall 2014 Swarthmore College" (unpublished data file, 2014).

19. Ibid.

20. Ibid. National Association of College Stores, *Student Watch Survey 2015–16 Key Findings* (National Association of College Stores, 2016), 1; Jasmine Woodson, *Reading Preferences Survey Write-Up* (Swarthmore, PA: Swarthmore College Libraries, 2014; unpublished data file), 103, 110, 113–14.

21. National Association of College Stores, "Student Watch Data Fall 2014 Swarthmore College" (unpublished data file, 2014).

22. Scott Gilbert, e-mail message to author, July 5, 2016.

23. Ibid.

Bibliography

Aydelotte, Frank. *Breaking the Academic Lock Step: The Development of Honors Work in American Colleges and Universities.* New York: Harper & Brothers, 1944.

Brooks, Robert C. *Reading for Honors at Swarthmore: A Record of the First Five Years, 1922–1927.* New York: Oxford University Press, 1927, p. 21.

"College Debating." *The Phoenix.* October 12, 1915. http://triptych.brynmawr.edu/cdm/ref/collection/SC_Phoenix/id/5791.

"Events Menu: Textbook Costs." *The Phoenix*, November 12, 2009. http://triptych.brynmawr .edu/cdm/ref/collection/SC_Phoenix/id/30675.

Hou, Linda. "Forum Addresses Textbook Issues." *The Phoenix* 35, no. 12 (November 19, 2009): 3. http://triptych.brynmawr.edu/cdm/ref/collection/SC_Phoenix/id/30675.

"ISCU." *The Phoenix*. March 13, 1962. http://triptych.brynmawr.edu/cdm/ref/collection/ SC_Phoenix/id/14854.

Lee, Allie. "Cheaper Online Textbook Options Not Popular." *Daily Gazette*, October 7, 2008.

National Association of College Stores. "Student Watch Data Fall 2014 Swarthmore College" (unpublished data file, 2014).

———. *Student Watch Survey 2015–16 Key Findings.* 2016, p. 1.

Section 133. Higher Education Opportunity Act, Pub. L. No. 110–315, 122 Stat. 3107 (August 14, 2008). https://www.gpo.gov/fdsys/pkg/PLAW-110pub1315/pdf/PLAW -110pub1315.pdf.

Swarthmore College. "Swarthmore College Financial Aid Statistics." *College Fact Book.* Swarthmore, PA: Swarthmore College, 2016. www.swarthmore.edu/sites/default/files/ assets/documents/institutional-research/FAStats.pdf.

———. *Strategic Directions for Swarthmore College.* Swarthmore, PA: Swarthmore College, 2011. http://sp.swarthmore.edu/wp-content/uploads/2012/01/StratPlan_Booklet _12e3.pdf.

Swarthmore College Faculty. *An Adventure in Education: Swarthmore College under Frank Aydelotte.* New York: Macmillan, 1941, p. 141.

Woodson, Jasmine. *Reading Preferences Survey Write-Up.* Swarthmore, PA: Swarthmore College Libraries, 2014 (unpublished datafile), 103, 110, 113–14.

THE GOOD AND THE BAD

Implementing a Textbook Reserve Program

Renee LeBeau-Ford and Joanna Ewing

Academic libraries are facing increasing demands to assess how they contribute to recruitment, retention, graduation, and student success. At the University of Central Arkansas' Torreyson Library, we feel strongly that implementing a college textbook reserve program is one potential answer to this ongoing challenge. The rising costs associated with pursuing higher education undoubtedly have a significant impact on student success and retention. In fact, some students have been forced to withdraw from classes if they are unable to afford the basic materials that they need, including textbooks. In addition to providing access to secondary source materials in a variety of subject areas, libraries can help alleviate these costs by providing copies of textbooks that can be used in the library for limited periods of time. Providing textbooks can help alleviate financial and emotional stress, which ultimately affects the students' ability to complete coursework. We have found that a combination of purchasing textbooks and pulling existing titles off of the main shelves for reserve provides a valuable and convenient service for our students.

In 2009, the Student Government Association passed a student and faculty-supported student library fee of $3 per credit hour at our university. Among the proposed ideas for using the fee was the capability of students to borrow textbooks. Academic libraries have not traditionally purchased textbooks, and we decided that we needed to address why this has been the case. There are three prevailing arguments against academic libraries purchasing textbooks. The most debated issue is the impact on the library's budget. With academic library budgets shrinking and the cost of materials increasing, why would library staff want to purchase expensive textbooks and decrease the overall buying power of the library's budget? Faculty may also express concern if they perceive investing in textbooks as taking away from the library's departmental purchasing. A second argument pertains to the textbooks themselves. If the library provided a textbook, would students be less likely to purchase or rent it themselves? Could this possibly affect student progress within the class? Finally, a third concern is how a textbook reserve collection would impact the library's staffing needs and existing workflows. In this chapter, we will discuss how these concerns were addressed at our library.

The library began the textbook reserve with several goals in mind. From the beginning, the library stated that the objective of the textbook program was to provide supplemental access to textbooks rather than to replace their purchase. We wanted to make sure that students did not fall behind at the beginning of the semester if their financial aid was delayed or they were short on funds. The program was designed to provide an alternative to students hauling heavy books around all day, as well as to reduce the potential stress of leaving a book at home when a student may need it on campus. We were also aware that students were frequently unsuccessfully requesting textbooks via interlibrary loan, so providing copies within the library would afford them a faster alternative.

After seven years of implementing our textbook reserve program, we would like to share our experiences and the lessons we have learned along the way. It is not our objective to discuss why the costs of college textbooks have dramatically increased or the controversy over textbooks in academic libraries. Instead, we aim to illustrate that despite the challenges of this textbook reserve program, the positive feedback we have received from both students and faculty has made it worthwhile and has contributed to student success.

PRE-PROJECT THOUGHTS

Before we implemented our textbook program, we needed to think though the details:

Selection   How much money did we need to get started? What books should we select?

Acquisitions   Would the campus bookstore be willing to work with us? Would we save money using online retailers?

Cataloging and processing   Should we create a unique catalog location for the textbook program? What should be the timeline for processing?

Access   How long should the checkout period be? How should we address overdue items? Should we charge fines?

Marketing   How should we publicize the collection to students and faculty?

Assessment   How do we judge the effectiveness of the program?

SELECTION AND ACQUISITIONS

The first step in building a textbook collection is deciding how much money you want to spend and what materials are going to be purchased. Here at Torreyson Library, we are fortunate to have the aforementioned student library fee, which generates over $800,000 per year for the library. The Library Committee, consisting of faculty and student representatives, provides input on how the funds should be spent. Since its beginning, the fee has been primarily used for extended library hours and renovation projects. One of the many smaller projects funded by this fee has been the textbook reserve program. The students from the committee requested and approved spending up to $10,000 per year annually on textbooks. The students later agreed that the textbook reserve collection was so beneficial that they approved of the library spending any amount it felt necessary. As a result, textbooks have accounted for approximately 5–7 percent of the library's total book budget over the last few years. Using the library fee to purchase textbooks has ensured that the library's original budget is not used for textbooks and departmental needs are not overlooked in favor of textbook purchases.

TERM	CLASS	COURSE	CRN	INSTR	ISBN	AUTHOR	TITLE	EDITION	REQ/ REC	NEW PRICE	USED PRICE	RENTAL PRICE
SUM	BIOL	1400	30022	Smith	9.78..	PEPPERS	BIOL 1400/1401/1402 LAB MANUAL	2015–2016	REQ	37.95	0	0
SUM	BIOL	1400	30033	Smith	9.78..	SINGH–CUNDY	DISCOVER BIOLOGY	5TH 2012	REQ	143.95	113.95	29.95
SUM	BIOL	1400	30033	Jones	9.78..	PEPPERS	BIOL 1400/1401/1402 LAB MANUAL	2015–2016	REQ	37.95	0	0
SUM	BIOL	1400	30149	White	9.78..	PEPPERS	BIOL 1400/1401/1402 LAB MANUAL	2015–2016	REQ	37.95	0	0
SUM	BIOL	1400	30149	White	9.78..	SINGH–CUNDY	DISCOVER BIOLOGY	5TH 2012	REQ	143.95	113.95	29.95

Figure 3.1 | Unedited Version of Textbook Spreadsheet from Campus Bookstore

Toward the end of each semester, we request a list of all textbooks to be used during the next term from the campus bookstore. This initial spreadsheet can be sorted to reflect courses with multiple sections or those in which instructors are using the same text. Figure 3.1 shows a sample of the types of course and textbook information we receive from the bookstore. This spreadsheet is edited to eliminate duplicate or unnecessary information before it is distributed (see the "Access" section later in this chapter for more information).

We initially selected freshman and sophomore-level courses in which enrollment was traditionally high and/or numerous instructors were using the same textbook. As we accommodated these lower-level courses, we began to expand into some upper-level materials. In the beginning, the manager of the campus bookstore would let us know if they were running low on a particular book. We would then purchase the last copy of that title, thereby providing access to a potentially wider audience.

Selection has evolved over time into a collaborative affair, with requests coming directly from the faculty and the Circulation Department. At the beginning of each semester, our first priority has always been to purchase textbooks used by multiple sections or instructors. During the first two weeks of a semester we will purchase items that have been requested by faculty and students. Staff at the circulation desk take textbook requests and send them to Acquisitions daily. When taking a request, it is imperative that staff communicate to students that there is no guarantee that a particular book will be purchased.

Books were initially purchased via our campus bookstore because we believed this would provide easier tracking and statistical gathering. However, we found that the bookstore tended to receive textbooks just before the start of each semester, which did not allow us enough time to select, purchase, and process items before the first day of classes. By the second year of our textbook program, we were ordering almost everything weeks in advance from online book retailers and only ordering the last-minute items from the campus bookstore.

We have encountered two unique issues with ordering textbooks online. One issue is that arrival dates for items can be problematic. For instance, when purchasing items in December for the following semester, several of our items did not arrive until after we returned from the holiday break and only a day before classes were to begin. We have also learned to look carefully when purchasing really inexpensive items online. One time, we accidentally purchased a textbook with a cover label that read "Restricted! For sale in India,

Bangladesh, Nepal, Pakistan, Sri Lanka and Bhutan." If a deal sounds too good to be true, it probably is. There is still controversy over the use of "international editions" in the academic world, and our library has decided not to add these editions to our textbook collection. Our goal is to provide the exact editions that instructors require for their courses, and international editions are not always the same as their American counterparts.

One very useful discovery that we made as time passed was that students were finding some of their textbooks within our regular collection. By the third year of our textbook reserve program, we started actively pulling books from the library shelves that were also on the bookstore's list, including classic novels like *The House on Mango Street* and *Behind the Beautiful Forevers*. To our surprise, we also discovered that some titles we had purchased from faculty recommendations or general acquisitions were now being used as textbooks. Examples of these included a handbook for multimedia editing and a neuroscience textbook. If these texts were not pulled for reserve, the first student to discover them in the catalog was likely the only person who would be able to use them for the semester.

We have learned over time that using online retailers allows us to purchase and process items earlier than the campus bookstore, while the bookstore is useful for last-minute purchases and campus custom editions. Online ordering also allows for the convenience and potential cost savings of purchasing used copies. However, it can be difficult to return items purchased online, and shipments are sometimes delayed. We have also learned that the timing of textbook availability is very important. When a student requests a textbook on the first or second day of class and we do not have it, that student will most likely not ask for it again.

CATALOGING AND PROCESSING OF TEXTBOOKS

Like most aspects of our textbook collection, our library's cataloging and processing activities have changed over time as a result of lessons learned. One major challenge we faced when we first began implementing this program was to establish an efficient workflow that would allow the textbooks to become available to students as quickly as possible (see figure 3.2). We discovered early on that students would call or come to the library looking for their textbooks as soon as they received their syllabi. This information helped them decide

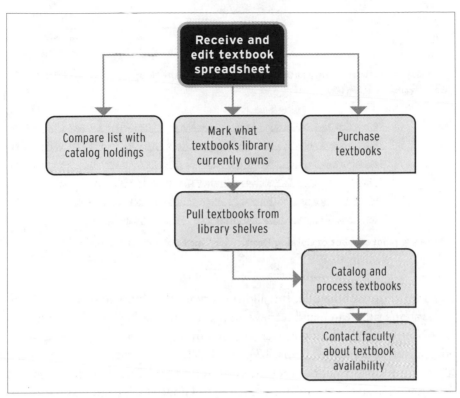

Figure 3.2 | **Textbook Collection Workflow**

which textbooks they might need to buy themselves. As we previously noted, students only ask about a title once. If we do not have the book when they ask for it, they are not likely to return and ask again. Therefore, we decided to be more proactive in our textbook purchasing and processing so that these items would be ready before students start asking about them.

Once we received new textbooks to be added to the collection, we also faced a challenge to ensure that they were processed and cataloged in a timely manner. While most of our acquisitions are not needed immediately, textbooks required higher priority to get them on the shelves faster. All textbooks are now cataloged and processed as soon as possible after receipt. This is particularly important for students who may be looking for these items, as order records are promptly added to our library catalog after items have been purchased.

To assist with locating textbooks that have been ordered but not yet cataloged, we enter textbook order records into the system a little differently than other order records. For each item we place the letters "TBR" (Textbook

| | | TITLE ▼ | tbr |

☐ Limit search to ava

Result Page 1 [2]

🔄 **Add Marked to Folder** 🔄 **Add All On Page** 📋 **Add Marked to My Lists**

Num	Mark	TITLES (1-50 of 114)
1	☐	TBR: A Concise Introduction To Logic (Book And CD - ROM) - 9TH. ED. [AMAZON] : Hurley
2	☐	TBR: A Topical Approach To Lifespan Development - 8TH. Revised ED. (ALIBRIS) : Santro
3	☐	TBR: American English - Dialects And Variation (3RD. REV. ED.) [ALIBRIS] : Wolfram, Wal
4	☐	TBR: An Introduction To Policing - 8TH. Revised ED. (ALIBRIS) : Forst, Linda
5	☐	TBR: Analyzing American Democracy - Politics And Political Science (2ND. ED.) : Bond, J
6	☐	TBR: Assembly Language For X86 Processors - 6TH. ED. (ALIBRIS) : Kip, R. Irvine

Figure 3.3 | **Screenshot of Catalog Results for Textbook Order Records**

Reserve) in front of the title. This allows everyone the ability to type "TBR" into our system's title search and retrieve an up-to-date list of what new textbooks have been ordered, where they were ordered from, and most importantly, which edition was ordered (see figure 3.3). This has been a tremendous help for the Cataloging Department as they attempt to find the correct order record and for circulation staff and students who need to know which textbooks have been ordered but may not yet be available for use.

Another challenge has emerged regarding generating statistics for the composition and use of the textbook collection. Library professionals recognize the importance of maintaining accurate circulation statistics to illustrate the use of library resources. When we began our textbook program, catalogers chose to categorize these textbooks under the generic catalog location of "Course Reserves." This category included both textbooks that were being used by multiple sections of a course (such as a general biology textbook) and items that individual instructors may be using in particular sections (such as a DVD about genetic engineering). However, we discovered that it was difficult to differentiate between the circulation rates of the different types of items within this category when generating statistics. Therefore, we decided to create a new "Textbook Reserve" catalog location to separate out the books used in multiple course sections. This new designation has since made statistical analysis of the collection much easier.

Transitioning the textbook collection between semesters is another challenge that requires careful planning and coordination between Cataloging,

Acquisitions, and Circulation. For instance, frequently a title is used only in the fall semester, but not in the spring. The library has to decide what to do with books not currently used by classes. We have chosen to keep those books on reserve since they will likely be used the following semester.

We have learned a number of lessons concerning the cataloging and processing of textbooks. Textbooks should receive high priority for cataloging and processing so that they will be available for students as soon as possible. Limiting the number of staff involved in working with handling these items makes the process run much more smoothly, both in initially adding items to the collection and transitioning between semesters. Adding an easily recognizable code to textbook order records facilitates locating them to attach to their corresponding bibliographic records. It is also a good idea to create a special catalog location for the textbook location to make both searching and statistical analysis easier.

ACCESS

The textbook reserve collection is located behind the circulation desk, and students can check out these items to use within the library for two-hour periods. Therefore, it is no surprise that starting the textbook program has made a significant impact on activity at the circulation desk. When our library's collection mainly consisted of regular books and multimedia materials, circulation desk activity was slow enough that its staff could briefly step away from the desk to assist with computer or copier issues. However, introducing other items to the collection such as laptops, other small equipment including headphones and calculators, and textbooks has completely changed the amount of interactions at the circulation desk. Figure 3.4 illustrates that the total circulation of the textbook reserve collection has increased over time.

In addition to quantity, the textbook collection has also changed the nature of circulation desk activity as well. Circulation staff members are now increasingly fielding textbook requests such as "I need that red book" or "I need the book with the eye on it," which can be quite puzzling when dealing with a growing textbook collection. Likewise, students usually ask for textbooks by course number (i.e., Writing 1320) or professor name rather than the Library of Congress call numbers by which they are organized.

In an effort to address these issues, we created an Excel spreadsheet based upon the campus bookstore's textbook list that includes the course numbers

	2013-2014 (%)	2014-2015 (%)	2015-2016 (%)
Textbook Reserves	9.5	9.8	13.5
Books	23.5	22.0	22.5
Laptops, Calculators	52.3	56.8	54.2
Audio/Visual	9.6	8.6	7.8
ILL and Other Misc.	5.2	2.7	2.0
TOTAL CIRCULATION	100.0%	100.0%	100.0%

Figure 3.4 | **Textbook Collection Circulation Activity 2013-2016**

CALL NUMBER	CLASS	COURSE	AUTHOR	TITLE	EDITION
DO NOT OWN	BIOL	1400	PEPPERS	BIOLOGY 1400/1401/1402 LAB MANUAL	2015-2016
QH308.2 D57 2012	BIOL	1400	SINGH-CUNDY	DISCOVER BIOLOGY	5TH 2012

Figure 3.5 | **Sample Portion of Edited Textbook List**

and book titles for the textbooks that the library owns (see figure 3.5). Putting together this document each semester requires a good deal of "cleanup" to clarify incomplete course information listed on the bookstore's original spreadsheet, but it is extremely useful for staff assisting students with textbook questions. The spreadsheet is loaded onto the desktops of the circulation and reference desk computers, and e-mailed to the Financial Aid Office and other interested campus departments. Staff can then use Excel's "find" feature to easily look up course or textbook information within the spreadsheet before searching for the book in our system. We encourage students to bring their course syllabi with them to the library when looking for their textbooks. This makes the search process much more efficient, particularly if the student seeks a generic title or specific edition.

MARKETING

Over the last few years we have publicized our textbook collection through social media, newsletters, instructional sessions, faculty e-mails, campus tours, and word of mouth. It is impossible to ascertain the impact of each method or which method best reaches students. However, we believe that word of mouth and faculty announcements are how most students discover our textbook collection. During recruitment tours, campus student ambassadors have been told to highlight our textbook collection and extended hours, along with other information. It is amazing when we instead hear them tell prospective students that "the library has all of your textbooks" and "the library never closes." This indicates an area where further training may be necessary.

In the third year of our textbook program, we decided to begin e-mailing each of the departments with personalized lists of which textbooks were being offered for that department (see the sample e-mail below). This was time-consuming, but worthwhile. We received a lot of positive feedback from faculty, as well as requests for additional textbook purchases. A few faculty members donated their personal copies to add to the collection once they were aware of its existence.

This semester the Torreyson Library has the following Accounting Textbooks on Textbook Reserve at the Circulation Desk. Please let your students know that they may check titles out for a 2 hour period to be used in the library.

ACCT 2310

Horngren's Financial and Managerial Accounting, 4th edition, 2014.

ACCT 2322

Business Law Today, 2014

ACCT 3311

Intermediate Accounting, 15th edition

ACCT 4312

Advanced Financial Accounting, 10th edition, 2014

Please contact me directly if you have any questions regarding the library's Textbook Reserve Program.

ASSESSMENT

How does an institution assess whether or not its textbook reserve program is effective? Torreyson Library staff members have received positive verbal feedback from students regarding our textbook program since its implementation, but we wanted to get a better idea of which students were utilizing these resources and why they were doing so. We decided to put together a short five-question anonymous survey to give to students as they were checking out textbooks at the circulation desk for one week during the spring 2016 semester. Although we did not have a preferred sample size in mind due to this survey's informal nature, we were pleased to received eighty-three total responses equally distributed between undergraduate classifications. Survey results revealed that student use of our textbook collection is due to a combination of both financial and convenience factors.

Student comments on the survey also indicated that they are extremely satisfied with the textbook program, and that many rely on it to assist them with their college expenses (see figure 3.6). We recognize that this perceived

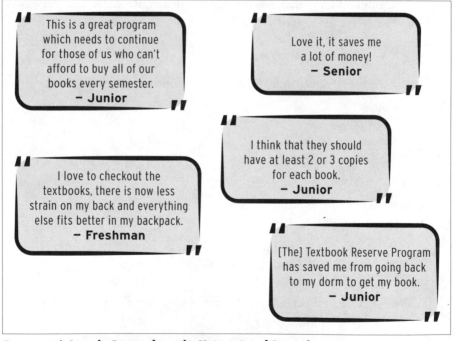

Figure 3.6 | **Sample Quotes from the University of Central Arkansas' Textbook Reserve Use Student Survey**

dependence is a source of increasing concern among some groups. However, we feel that providing students with limited access to class materials in the library is better than them not having access at all. Our future assessment plans include revising the survey to get a better idea of how, why, and by whom the textbook collection is being used. We would also like to extend the time period of the survey to see how collection use changes over time.

The collection's popularity is also reflected by its extremely high usage statistics. For example, one chemistry textbook has been checked out 525 times since August 2014. Overall use of the textbook collection has almost doubled in the past two years, and currently comprises 13.5 percent of our total materials checkouts. Library staff should discuss desired outcomes and assessment methods before implementing a new textbook reserve collection. For instance, we have learned that retrieving usage data can be difficult if catalog locations or item types are not clearly defined.

FUTURE THOUGHTS

As we move forward, we have a few continuing questions to consider:

Funding Is this model financially sustainable? Should we seek campus or external funding? Should we reaffirm with the Student Government Association that they still support this program?

Access How do we address the issue of late returns without charging students? (We do not charge fines at our institution.) Should we set up a holds system for textbooks? How can we more efficiently collect data on heavily used items for additional purchasing decisions? Can our new discovery service assist with access?

Marketing How we can better publicize our textbook collection to the student body? Do students understand the evolving nature of the collection? Can we partner with the Student Government Association to conduct a more comprehensive student-wide textbook survey?

Assessment What types of data should we collect? How often should we collect the data? How can we distinguish between one individual repeatedly using the same book and multiple individuals using that same book? What other ways can we use the data besides the library's annual report?

CONCLUSION

Every year at most universities and colleges, administrators spend hours calculating the upcoming year's tuition, room, board, and fees. Great discussion is put into whether or not tuition and fees should be raised one, two, three, or five percent. If tuition were $6,000 per semester for the average student, an increase could amount to anywhere from $60 to $300. How will this affect the students? Will they not enroll? Will they drop out? Who is looking at the cost of the textbooks each semester?

The 2012 Florida Student Textbook Survey of over 22,000 college students concluded that textbooks play a major role in whether or not a student enrolls, remains, or succeeds in a class. Among their findings were that

- 64 percent did not purchase the required textbook
- 45 percent did not register for a class because of textbook cost
- 21 percent withdrew from a course due to textbook cost

Pictured below (see figure 3.7) is a sample of five textbooks (with a total cost of around $796) that may be required for a business student during one semester. We argue that this small investment may be the deciding factor in a student's academic success, enrollment, or retention.

According to a report published by the Student Public Interest Research Group titled "Covering the Cost: Why We Can No Longer Ignore the High Price of Textbooks," textbook prices increased 1,041 percent from January 1977 to June 2015, or 73 percent since 2006.[1] Within our library, the price

Figure 3.7 | **Selected Textbooks for the University of Central Arkansas**

of one typical Spanish textbook has increased 34.3 percent from the 2009 to 2017 editions. Shouldn't universities and colleges be looking at the cost of textbooks? Do rising textbook costs have a larger impact on students than tuition increases? Regardless of the answers to these questions, we believe that our textbook reserve program has contributed to student success by increasing the accessibility of course materials and decreasing students' financial burden.

While our textbook reserve program continues to evolve, we believe that we have managed to address the common concerns mentioned at the beginning of this chapter. We have become more proactive about figuring out which textbooks may already be in our circulating collection and pulling those titles before students can check them out. Our university's student body continues to be supportive of both the student library fee and the textbook collection, helping to ensure the reserve collection's longevity. Finally, having a limited number of staff involved in the processing of the collection and clearly communicating their concerns or suggestions has resulted in more efficient transitions between semesters. It may be challenging at first to establish a textbook collection, but we argue that the benefits to students far outweigh the difficulties.

Note

1. Ethan Senack and Robert Donoghue, "Covering the Cost: Why We Can No Longer Afford to Ignore High Textbook Prices," Student PIRGS, February 3, 2016, www.studentpirgs.org/reports/sp/covering-cost.

Bibliography

Senack, Ethan, and Robert Donoghue. "Covering the Cost: Why We Can No Longer Afford to Ignore High Textbook Prices." Student PIRGS. February 3, 2016. www.studentpirgs.org/reports/sp/covering-cost.

A STUDENT-FUNDED
TEXTBOOK RESERVE PROGRAM

Joanna Duy, Kirsten Huhn, and Dubravka Kapa

For the past six years Concordia University Library has been providing textbooks for all undergraduate courses via its course reserves service. Some 8,000 textbooks are on reserve each academic year for approximately 2,500 unique courses per semester. The textbook program grew out of a larger undergraduate students' initiative that uses a course fee levy to provide a budget for improved library services in areas they identified as priorities. In this chapter we will present the history and parameters of the textbook program. We will describe the workflows involved in providing a timely, seamless service that spans two campuses, and outline the complexity of developing an acquisition process that is initiated by faculty through the university bookstore. Furthermore, we will discuss the challenges in managing online discovery and physical access to the textbook collection, as well as the necessary de-selection process. Finally, we will provide a brief analysis of our reserves collection usage patterns.

OVERVIEW OF CONCORDIA UNIVERSITY

Concordia University is a large comprehensive university (27,792 full-time enrollments) located in Montreal, Quebec (Canada). The university has two campuses and two libraries. The larger R. Howard Webster Library, located on the downtown Sir George Williams campus, supports business, engineering, fine arts, and most humanities/social sciences disciplines, and the smaller Georges P. Vanier Library, located on the Loyola campus, serves sciences, psychology, journalism, communications, and applied human sciences.

The university has a large proportion (86 percent) of undergraduate students. There is no medical or law faculty. In line with the prevailing trends at other Quebec universities, the great majority of undergraduate students at Concordia are working to support their studies.[1]

Concordia Library has had a popular print course reserve service for many years. Until the 1990s the library, like many other North American academic libraries, was purchasing selected course textbooks, placing them in a protected course reserves collection, and making them available to students for short loan periods.

In the early 1990s the increase in the price of periodicals subscriptions, coupled with cuts to library funding, led to a decreased capacity for monograph acquisition.[2] Purchasing textbooks, which generally have a short life, was seen as further limiting the library's capacity to continue developing its monograph collection. Concordia Library therefore stopped buying course textbooks, with only an occasional textbook purchased upon faculty request.

The prices of textbooks for postsecondary education were high, particularly in certain disciplines, and were continuing to rise.[3] Realizing that purchasing textbooks significantly increases the cost of education (the cost of textbooks in Canada is approximately 20 percent of the tuition fee), and may present an obstacle for a successful academic career, especially for students with low incomes, some instructors donated copies of textbooks to the library to be used specifically as course reserves.[4]

Other instructors replaced textbooks with collections of selected chapters and articles and requested that multiple photocopies be kept in the library's course reserves collection for borrowing. Until June 2012 the Copyright Act of Canada did not recognize "fair dealing" in the educational context, and copyright fees applied to reserve materials. The university, therefore, had an agreement with Quebec's copyright agency (COPIBEC) which allowed instructors to make multiple copies of articles and chapters for use in a course or to place on reserve in the library. Copying for course reserves had to be done through the university's bookstore, which would then regulate copyright payments with COPIBEC. The payment of copyright fees was funded through a course levy that each student had to pay.

In addition to print reserves, which were offered at both campus libraries (depending on which campus was offering the course), the library introduced an electronic reserves service in 2004 to provide online access to articles, book chapters, and some e-books. Since then, the electronic reserves service has grown steadily, reaching approximately 8,000 digital items per semester in 2015–16.

STUDENT UNION TO THE RESCUE

In 2009, recognizing the impact of textbook prices on the cost of studies and the potential role of the library, the Concordia Student Union (CSU) executive started a conversation with the library to explore options for making textbooks available for borrowing. In November 2009, undergraduate students voted in a referendum to approve a "library services" contribution, a $1 per credit donation, for ten years, with the money going towards funding new services or improving existing ones. In addition to increasing the availability of textbooks and course packs in the library, students identified 24-hour access to the library, increased availability for free loan of laptops and netbooks, improved silent and quiet study zones, and additional study spaces in the Webster Library as services to be funded with their contribution.

In December 2009 the Concordia University Board of Governors approved the collection of the library services contribution. The Library Services Fund Agreement was finalized in April 2010, and the Library Services Fund Committee (LSFC) was established to oversee the stewardship of the fund. The LSFC consisted of four student representatives, a representative from the Office of Advancement and Alumni, and three library administrators plus the university librarian (who is the chair).

Concordia Library's acquisition of textbooks began in summer 2010. Each academic year the library purchases, on average, some 1,600 textbooks and other course materials (such as supplementary readings, DVDs, or CDs) from the CSU Library fund; the textbooks are purchased for the campus where the course is being held. The annual cost of acquiring all needed course materials is approximately $90,000 CAD (roughly $70,000 USD) per year. The current collection consists of some 8,000 items.

FINDING THE WAY

The existing course reserves service relied on faculty to inform the library which textbooks to put on reserve for which course. However, with the new student-funded model, the scale of the service was about to change dramatically. From some 300 courses, the library was now committed to managing textbooks for approximately 2,500 courses per semester. Making sure that the library identified and acquired textbooks and course packs for all undergraduate courses was thus a large and complex new challenge.

The University Bookstore was the obvious place to look for textbook adoption data. The bookstore was already compiling this information from instructors in order to have the books and course packs ready for students to purchase at the beginning of a semester. Thus the library approached the bookstore to start exploring ways to make this information available and usable for the library's nascent course reserves service.

TECHNICAL SERVICES PROCESSES

Working out and streamlining effective procedures to translate the distinctive bookstore data into data that could be used for regular acquisitions and technical services processes in the library system was one of the more complex challenges for the Technical Services Department. Once a week, throughout the year, Technical Services staff receive an e-mail from the bookstore liaison with the list of books that have been adopted by instructors, along with information about the course, campus location, and expected enrollment (Textbooks Adoptions Report, or Bookstore Report). The report is received in tab-separated values (.tsv) format and is immediately reformatted by library staff into Excel spreadsheets. It took a couple of semesters of defining spreadsheets and fine-tuning macros and other tools until we established a smooth processing of the Textbooks Adoptions Reports.

The processed list of the Bookstore Report is checked against our integrated library system (Sierra by Innovative) to see if copies of the textbooks already exist in the library's collections before proceeding with the purchase. During this process, graduate course textbooks, loose-leaf materials, student manuals, and lab books, as well as e-textbooks sold with a single-user access are removed.

At first we tested various options in trying to establish an automated process of checking existing holdings and copies in our ILS, but in the end there were too many gaps and inconsistencies (e.g., incomplete, abbreviated, or otherwise ambiguous book titles; missing ISBN digits; missing author or publication year) in the Bookstore Reports to ensure a reliable automated process. The weekly reports are now checked and annotated manually by staff. For a few weeks leading up to the start of a new semester, when most professors communicate their textbook choices, the lists can be several hundred items long, making the manual checking of holdings for each title a significant staff time commitment. Despite our efforts, we have not yet been able to automate our checking process. That said, due diligence in checking each item on the Textbook Adoptions Report is crucial because on average 80 percent of items on the list are already in the library collection and do not need to be bought.

The library orders each title that is not already available in its collection, including titles where the library owns a different edition. The library also purchases a copy of each course pack available in the bookstore. Initially, since the total cost of this new comprehensive service was unknown, the Library Services Fund Committee decided to make available only one copy of a course textbook and then assess its use and cost. Early on it became clear that one copy might not always be enough to meet the student demand. Reserves staff reported that a number of textbooks were constantly signed out, causing student frustration. Pairing the titles in high demand with the class enrollment data in the report showed that they corresponded to classes with 150 or more students. A decision was therefore made to add another copy whenever a total enrollment (e.g., in all sections of one course, or in all classes that use the same title) reaches 175 (an average number of students in bigger classes). The exception are textbooks in LC call number P, which had a very low usage that did not warrant purchasing a second copy (see the section on "Use Data" later in this chapter). A third copy is ordered in rare cases where a course has an enrollment of 290 students or more. For even larger classes, Acquisitions staff use their judgment to determine the number of copies to buy. The "right" number of copies for each class is difficult to determine from the enrollment data only, so the number of copies is further adjusted based on information from front-line reserves staff. An even more specific approach to determining the appropriate number of copies should be based on analyzing textbooks borrowing data.

After the Bookstore Report is reviewed and annotated by technical services staff, it is then turned into an order file that is sent back to the bookstore, effectively placing orders for all items as indicated on the file. Approximately 90 percent of textbooks and all course packs are purchased directly from the bookstore. The library receives no discounts for the material purchased from the bookstore, but pays no additional sales taxes or shipping fees. A much smaller number of titles (fewer than fifty) is purchased from Concordia's Co-op Bookstore, a not-for-profit alternative campus bookstore that is the preferred option for textbook orders for some professors. While the process of dealing with course materials from the Co-op Bookstore is much less streamlined than the regular bookstore adoptions, we are also dealing with a negligible number of titles through this route. In exceptional circumstances, the library will place last-minute rush orders for course materials through online booksellers such as Amazon.ca. This is largely the case for titles that are ordered as replacements or additional copies later on in the semester when they are no longer in stock at the bookstore. Due to higher costs, both in material pricing and staff time, we try to avoid this route as much as possible.

In addition to serving as the basis of the order file, the processed Bookstore Report has two other functions. Further processed into a text (.txt) file, it is used to automatically create the batch of brief bibliographic records, item records, and order records in the library system. It is also sent to course reserves assistants for processing physical items for the reserve collection.

Bibliographic, item, and order records with data automatically derived from the Bookstore Report are set up for each title according to our regular parameters at the point of order. In the order records, the library enters a Title ID# field with the bookstore's item stock number, as well as a Note field that contains a summary of course information based on the information provided in the bookstore file. Adding the bookstore stock number facilitates invoice matching, and makes up for the lack of a library purchase order number on the invoices. The data in the order record Note field (course number and section, the semester and campus location of the course, the abbreviated course title, the instructor's name, and the enrollment) is used when creating the course reserve record.

The bookstore sends shipments of textbooks and course materials weekly. The bookstore also informs library staff about canceled courses, and makes sure any library orders for those courses are canceled accordingly. The received material is then paid for, cataloged, and physically prepared for course reserves in the rush-processing workflow, giving it priority over any other library materials in the processing stream. With the exception of course packs, all course materials are fully cataloged and assigned a Library of Congress call number. All records are fully indexed and searchable, displaying in the library catalog and our discovery layer. Notably, for all items purchased with CSU Library funds, a local MARC field 983 ("Unique collections index") is added in all

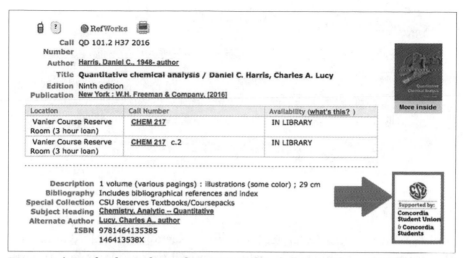

Figure 4.1 | **Textbook Display with CSU Virtual Bookplate in Library Catalog**

bibliographic records. It serves to display a virtual bookplate indicating that the book was purchased using the CSU Library fund (see figure 4.1).

On average, the turnaround time for course reserve materials is about two weeks from the point of receipt of the bookstore file until the item goes on the shelf. In some cases it might take longer. The library has made an effort to communicate processes and procedures to the CSU. For example, the associate university librarian for collection services attends regular meetings of the LSFC to provide updates, answer any questions about processes and procedures, and hear students' feedback.

THE RESERVE ROOMS

To maximize the accessibility of the textbook collection, reserve rooms housing all course materials were established in both libraries. The construction of the rooms was funded by the Library Services Fund. These rooms are equipped with self-checkout machines and each room has its own security gate. In addition, there is a computer where users can look up items in the catalogue and/or reserve system, a photocopier/scanner, and a few tables and chairs for quick consultation.

When designing and planning these rooms, the goal was to make the course reserves collection as open and accessible to students as possible. Previously, this collection had been shelved behind the circulation desk and therefore was

| Professor/instructor | COURSE TEXTBOOKS | | | |
| Course | AHSC 312 | | | |

Materials for this Course			
Title	Author	Call #	Format
Human sexuality in a world of diversity / Spencer A. Rathus ... [et al.]	Rathus, Spencer A	Vanier Course Reserve Room (3 hour loan) -- AHSC 312 -- IN LIBRARY	
Human sexuality in a world of diversity / Spencer A. Rathus, Jeffrey S. Nevid, Lois Fichner-Rathus, Alexander McKay	Rathus, Spencer A., author	Vanier Course Reserve Room (3 hour loan) -- AHSC 312 -- IN LIBRARY	
Understanding human sexuality / Janet Shibley Hyde, John D. DeLamater, E. Sandra Byers	Hyde, Janet Shibley	Vanier Course Reserve Room (3 day loan) -- PSYC 297S -- IN LIBRARY	
Understanding human sexuality / Janet Shibley Hyde, University of Wisconsin-Madison, John D. DeLamater, University of Wisconsin-Madison, E. Sandra Byers, University of New Brunswick	Hyde, Janet Shibley, author	Vanier Course Reserve Room (3 hour loan) -- AHSC 312 -- IN LIBRARY	
Working in groups : communication principles and strategies / Isa N. Engleberg and Dianna R. Wynn	Engleberg, Isa N	Vanier Course Reserve Room (3 hour loan) -- AHSC 232 -- IN LIBRARY	

Figure 4.2 | **Course Record in the Library Catalog**

available only during desk service hours. The collection was shelved in Library of Congress call number order, which required that students find the call number before requesting the book from library staff. The service staff noticed that students would often give their course code instead of the call number, so in the reserve rooms we decided to shelve the collection by course code. This enables students to walk into the room and browse material available for their course without needing to check the catalog first.

Shelving items by course code works well for situations where a textbook is on reserve for a single course. Deciding how to shelve when the same title is used by more than one course was a challenge. For example, if book A is on reserve for BIOL 213 and CHEM 234, do we shelve all the copies under one course or do we shelve a copy under each course code? When we place one copy under each course, if a student is looking for a book in the BIOL 213 shelving section and the book has been checked out, the student will not realize that another copy is available under CHEM 234. Placing all the copies in one location under one course code and providing a dummy in the other ensures that a student will be aware of the availability of any copy.

It was decided to shelve all copies of the same book under one course. In the catalog, the title will display under both courses with the call number of the course it is shelved under (see figure 4.2).

Approximately 23 percent of our reserve books are cross-listed under more than one course code. However, this number may be somewhat inflated as a result of multiple factors, including alternate course codes being assigned to the same course and the way we manage our processing of course reserves.

Since opening in 2010, the reserve rooms have used a service model that is a mix of staff presence and self-service, with an increasing move towards

Figure 4.3 | **The Reserve Room at Vanier Library**

the latter. The Webster Library Reserve Room opened in 2010 as a "stand-alone" room located at some distance from the circulation desk, and requires staffing an additional service point. At least one staff member is scheduled to work at the desk in the room during service hours, and another staff member is assigned to check in and shelve returned items. The reserve room at the Webster Library is open only during staff service hours. The Vanier Library Reserve Room, which opened in 2015, is adjacent to the circulation desk (see figure 4.3) so that staff serving at the circulation desk could also help students in the reserve room when needed. The reserve room is in close proximity to the security agent who is stationed in the library during non-staffed hours, and who can intervene if the alarm goes off. This is ideal for overnight hours when there are no library staff present while the room remains open.

LOAN POLICIES AND FINES

The default loan period for textbooks is three hours, and 91 percent of our textbooks have this loan period. However, instructors can request that either a one-day or three-day loan apply; items with these loan periods account for

5 percent and 4 percent of the collection, respectively. In addition to instructor requests, library reserves staff may decide to keep superseded editions of textbooks, which are still popular, on reserve with a longer loan period as well.

The fine for reserves items that have not been returned on time is $2.00 CAD per hour or day, depending on whether the item is on an hourly or daily loan, up to a maximum of $20.00 CAD. When the fine reaches the maximum (e.g., after ten hours for hourly loans), a final overdue notice is sent to the user warning him that he will be charged a nonrefundable fee for replacement of the item. If the item is not returned the next day, we bill the user and place an order for a replacement copy. This model has worked well to keep the instances of users holding on to textbooks beyond their due date acceptably low.

USE DATA

Since 2011–12, the library has had on average 99,408 checkouts of reserve items per year. This value has remained fairly constant over five years, while the number of checkouts for non-reserve monographs has decreased significantly, as shown in figure 4.4.

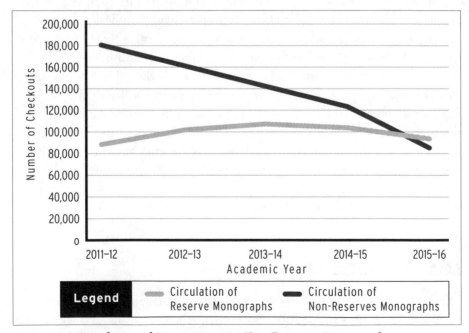

Figure 4.4 | **Circulation of Reserves versus Non-Reserves Monographs**

Borrowing data for our reserve material suggests that textbooks in certain disciplines are borrowed more than in others. For example, textbooks in science and technology circulate on average 24 times per semester, while textbooks in the humanities (LC call number ranges P, E, F, for example) circulate on average only 2–4 times per semester. In addition, only 20 percent of science and technology textbooks did not circulate at all, compared to over 50 percent in the humanities. Use also appears to be correlated with the cost of the textbook, with higher-cost items showing much higher use. These data would suggest that the library reserve collection is providing students with an appealing low-cost alternative to purchasing costly textbooks. Other data have suggested that as textbook costs increase, students are more likely to seek lower-cost options to purchasing.[5]

In addition to the textbook reserve service, Concordia Libraries has also offered an electronic reserves service since 2004, and it is interesting to compare usage trends from both the print and the electronic service. The electronic reserves service provides online access to articles, book chapters, and some e-books. Unlike the textbook program, which is funneled via the bookstore, the electronic reserves service is driven by faculty requests made directly to the library. The goal of the electronic reserves service is to provide convenient access to various readings—regardless of whether they are print or born digital, part of the library's collection, free web materials, or from a faculty member's own collection—into one stable list of readings for students.

The number of items on electronic reserve has been growing steadily in recent years, from 5,091 items in 2010–11 to 9,383 items in the 2015–16 academic year. The use of electronic readings has also increased, and during the 2015–16 academic year we had just shy of 300,000 views of our electronic course materials. Unlike textbook use, which is heaviest in science and technology, the top ten readings in our electronic reserves systems for the winter 2016 term were for humanities and social sciences courses. Although the library manages both the textbook and the electronic reserves service, it has no involvement in the process of selecting materials for either service. Having well-developed textbook and electronic services provides a great opportunity to analyze potential trends and helps the library develop relevant support for teaching. A detailed comparison of courses and materials available through both services would be a good starting point to help us understand how these two services complement each other.

SECURITY

Overall, lost and/or stolen books have not been a problem since the inception of the textbook project. However, we did increase our security for reserves items by using tattle tape in addition to the security tape that is in the bar code tags.

In May 2016 an inventory was done of the reserve collections at the Webster and Vanier libraries. Figure 4.5 below shows the results.

	WEBSTER LIBRARY	VANIER LIBRARY	TOTAL
Number of reserve items	6,362	1,375	7,737
Number of reserve items declared lost	76	13	89
Percentage of the total reserve collection	1.2%	0.95%	1.15%

Figure 4.5 | **Results of Reserve Collection Inventory, May 2016**

DE-SELECTION

The number of books on reserve at any time since the full inception of the textbook project has been approximately 7,000–8,000 items. Approximately 1,600 items (1,000 course packs and 600 textbooks) are added to the reserve collection each year. The limited space of the reserve rooms—and our desire to maintain a current collection that reflects readings for current or recently taught courses—requires that we de-select regularly.

The annual de-selection process starts in May/June, after winter courses have finished. All course packs (approximately 1,000) are discarded and replaced each academic year. Any instructor's personal copy that was put on reserve is returned to the instructor at the end of the academic year. Textbooks purchased specifically for course reserves are kept on reserve for two years after the last academic year in which they were adopted. As some courses are not offered every year, this is to ensure that we do not discard items that might be needed every second year. It is important, with this policy, to honor instructors' requests to remove items that are no longer on reserve for their courses (which happens infrequently). For all textbooks, we ensure that the item has not had substantial use in the previous year; if it has, we keep it on reserve for another year. The items are then sent to the collections librarian to decide whether they should be returned to the stacks or de-selected. Criteria such as total circulation, circulation in the current year, and last checkout date are used for assessment.

The copies that are to be removed from the library's collection are placed on book trucks at the entrance to the library and are offered free to students at the beginning of the fall semester.

CONCLUSION

The student-funded course reserves service at Concordia University Library is part of a unique major collaborative project between the Student Union and the library. With the systematic acquisition of undergraduate textbooks and other course materials for student use, the library is able to expand its services offered to students in an area that directly affects student learning and which has been identified as a priority by the student body.

Ensuring that all undergraduate course materials are purchased by the library requires close coordination with the University Bookstore. Their willingness to establish a regular flow of information on course adoptions was central to getting this project off the ground quickly.

The reserve rooms on each campus have been appreciated by students since they make course materials not just available, but also easier to find. In our experience, it is important, when planning reserve room space needs, to allow for shelving space that can support more than one year's worth of course material. At Concordia Library, we de-select course materials every two years in an effort to keep the material current but also to manage existing shelf space. With more shelving capacity we would be able to consider de-selection every three years, which would be more relevant to the life cycle of textbooks and the recurrence of certain courses.

Since its inception in summer 2010, processes related to the course reserves workflow have undergone continuous tweaking and revision, which will certainly continue for the duration of the mandate. Usage trends are the main driver as the library reevaluates workflows and processes such as the 24-hour availability of the reserve collection at the Webster Library on the downtown campus or the current formula for the number of copies purchased per total enrollment. An automated mechanism for checking the weekly Textbook Adoptions Report against existing library holdings could further improve the efficiency of the technical services workflow. Changing the current practice of full cataloging could further speed up the process and reduce the current two weeks processing for this time-sensitive collection. To complement the current self-checkout option in both reserves rooms, we may explore student self-check-in.

All in all, while current usage is strong, we expect to see a downward trend in demand for print course materials over the next few years. Some preliminary analyses of usage patterns in our library points toward a rise of electronic reserves in tandem with a decreased use of print textbooks. In planning for the next four years—the remainder of the time on the current Library Services Fund Agreement—the library will continue to monitor and adapt the course reserves service, while at the same time striving to develop future service offers in line with the evolving needs of students.

Notes

1. Conseil Supérieur de l'Éducation du Québec, "Parce que les façons de réaliser un projet d'études universitaires ont changé . . . ," 2013, https://www.cse.gouv.qc.ca/fichiers/documents/publications/Avis/50–0480.pdf.
2. Association of Research Libraries, "Monograph and Serial Costs in ARL Libraries, 1986–2011," 2012, www.arl.org/storage/documents/monograph-serial-costs.pdf.
3. Janet Davison, "Back to School 2015: How Post-Secondary Students Can Fight 'Grim Reality' of Rising Textbook Costs," CBC News, 2015, www.cbc.ca/news/canada/back-to-school-2015-how-post-secondary-students-can-fight-grim-reality-of-rising-textbook-costs-1.3215013.
4. Government of Canada, Financial Consumer Agency of Canada, "Budget for Student Life: How Much Will Your Post-Secondary Education Cost?" 2014, www.fcac-acfc.gc.ca/Eng/forConsumers/lifeEvents/payingPostSecEd/Pages/Budgetfo-Unbudget.aspx#books.
5. Higher Education Strategy Associates, "Data on Textbook Costs," 2015, http://higheredstrategy.com/data-on-textbook-costs/.

Bibliography

Association of Research Libraries. "Monograph and Serial Costs in ARL Libraries, 1986–2011." 2012. www.arl.org/storage/documents/monograph-serial-costs.pdf.

Conseil Supérieur de l'Éducation du Québec. "Parce que les façons de réaliser un projet d'études universitaires ont changé. . . ." 2013. https://www.cse.gouv.qc.ca/fichiers/documents/publications/Avis/50–0480.pdf.

Davison, Janet. "Back to School 2015: How Post-Secondary Students Can Fight 'Grim Reality' of Rising Textbook Costs." CBC News. 2015. www.cbc.ca/news/canada/back-to-school-2015-how-post-secondary-students-can-fight-grim-reality-of-rising-textbook-costs-1.3215013.

Government of Canada, Financial Consumer Agency of Canada. "Budget for Student Life: How Much Will Your Post-Secondary Education Cost?" 2014. www.fcac-acfc .gc.ca/Eng/forConsumers/lifeEvents/payingPostSecEd/Pages/Budgetfo-Unbudget .aspx#books.

Higher Education Strategy Associates. "Data on Textbook Costs." 2015. http:// higheredstrategy.com/data-on-textbook-costs/.

5

BUILDING A STEM COLLECTION OF UNDERGRADUATE TEXTBOOKS

Pattie Piotrowski and Christine McClure

Textbooks are a perennial problem for academic libraries. At an institution such as the Illinois Institute of Technology (Illinois Tech) where science, technology, engineering, and mathematics (STEM), plus architecture and business are the core disciplines, textbooks are often priced significantly higher than in other disciplines, creating problems for students with tight budgets. In addition, Illinois Tech enrolls and graduates a large population of international students; international enrollment has hovered in the 40 percent range for the last decade. These students may come from countries with different practices and ideas about libraries and textbooks. However, it was previously established circulation policies and practices that were the real problems for Galvin Library, the institution's main campus library.

Prior to 2008, the library made an effort to assist our students with getting textbooks for their classes. Students were able to request textbooks through two different catalogs: a statewide consortial system of academic institutions known as I-Share, and also through interlibrary loan, which used WorldCat.

The statewide system allows for unmediated requests, while WorldCat is a mediated system, requiring library staff to place, track, and recall items.

While titles used as textbooks were available in both systems, the real problem created by borrowing them was with the due dates. The consortial system allowed for an initial checkout period of 3 or 4 weeks with up to 3 renewals. However, at that time in the mid-2000s, the system had yet to standardize borrowing policies, and renewal policies differed for individual institutions in the consortium. WorldCat, on the other hand, did have a standard checkout period of three weeks, but renewal was up to the individual owner, so not all books were renewed.

The Illinois Tech fall and spring semesters stretch across a period of sixteen weeks each. Students were borrowing textbooks that were never going to be renewed long enough to be able to keep them for an entire semester. The students' response was to simply keep the books as long as they needed, ignoring due dates, automated notifications, and direct staff appeals. Much staff time was invested in sending notifications about overdue or assumed lost books, with little return on that staff time. In 2006, just to cite one egregious example, over two semesters eight of the same textbook titles were replaced for lending institutions when our patrons never returned the books. Of course, we could charge the student's university account, but at that time there was no process or mechanism for library fees built into the student accounting process. Basically, we were paying for textbooks for our students.

In 2006–07 the library started changing lending policies and building a relationship with student accounting, as well as meeting with student groups on campus. Library staff in Circulation, Interlibrary Loan, and Reserves held a series of meetings in which lending policies were reviewed and ultimately updated or new policies were created.

To start, textbooks were no longer able to be requested through the mediated interlibrary loan system. In 2008 we signed up for ILLiad services, hosted by OCLC, which better automated the requesting, notification, and services for interlibrary loan. However, in 2007, since this was a mediated system with library staff reviewing and placing each request, the denial of textbook requests, and e-mails explaining the new policies still required much staff time. Interlibrary loan staff created e-mail templates to cut down on notification and explanation time, and this greatly reduced the necessary staff time dedicated to these functions, but it wasn't until the adoption of ILLiad that this process was truly automated and staff time drastically reduced.

For students who had experience with the unmediated system, there were few policy changes we could make, as students could make direct requests in the system that would be filled and shipped to our library. Therefore, the problems with the overdue or non-returned statuses of these books still existed, so we needed to look for better enforcement of payment policies for the library, and increase the student responsibility for non-returned books.

The assistant dean for public services, whose responsibilities included the Interlibrary Loan Department, worked closely with university accounting so that charges on a student's account for lost or non-returned books would generate a hold on getting a transcript, and charges beyond $300 could delay receipt of a student's diploma. The assistant dean also worked with librarians and library staff who did orientations for incoming students so that the library could better prepare student expectations regarding textbooks. An explanation for the student's responsibility for purchasing textbooks was worked into orientations, signage, and brochures that were handed out. A special research guide was developed for textbooks, and a link was placed on the library's home page explaining textbook policy. The last relationship to build on and expand was with student leadership organizations, such as the Student Government Association and the Union Board, to communicate the new borrowing policies on textbooks to students.

The tightening of these policies produced immediate results and strengthened the library's ability to be a good borrower within the consortium and interlibrary loan systems. However, it did little to endear the library to its patrons. With the price of textbooks reaching exorbitant levels—it was not unusual for a STEM textbook to cost a minimum of $200—students were caught in an expensive loop, and we heard of more and more students not purchasing the materials needed for class. As a member of the Retention Task Force (RTF), the assistant dean had the opportunity to speak about the problems that students were facing that had a real impact on their success. Also at the RTF table were university staff and administrators from Financial Aid, Student Affairs, Admission and Enrollment, and others. Initially, RTF members were about as split in opinion as the faculty were on the topic: some saw the negative impact on student success, while others felt textbooks have always been the responsibility of students and purchase should continue to be a student's obligation.

However, in 2008 the library received a set of questions from the administrator who managed Financial Aid and Admissions. He wondered how much it would cost the library to purchase a copy of every undergraduate textbook. In looking at textbooks and costs, library staff discovered that an initial purchase could top $55,000, or a full quarter of the library's print book collection budget. Searching the collection for books that could be removed from the circulating collection and placed on reserve as textbooks, and then actively soliciting departments and faculty for textbook copies, gave us a small but active reserve textbook collection. Before 2008 ended, the administrator who had questioned the cost of starting a textbook collection gave $25,000 in seed money to purchase new books for the collection. Thus, the undergraduate reserve textbook collection was officially introduced in spring 2009. The library continued to work with student groups to encourage donations of textbooks to the collection, and library staff continued to solicit textbooks from departments and faculty.

The library also needed to create new policies regarding the lending of the textbooks. In order to keep textbooks available and accessible to the largest number of students, one policy was that the books could be used only in the library. There are requests each semester from students, and even the occasional faculty member, when an exam is issued with a directive of notes and textbooks allowed. In that circumstance, we explain that the borrower can scan anything needed and take notes into the testing area, but the library cannot allow the book to leave the library. Another part of the policy limits the borrowing period to a two-hour loan limit. However, after returning the textbook, a patron is able to wait only fifteen minutes before borrowing the textbook again. This policy can be explained to patrons, because each loan is time-stamped. If a patron comes to borrow a textbook and it is already loaned out, the circulation staff can tell the patron when it is due back. For popular titles, that second borrower will often wait for the item to be returned, or leave and then return close to the time when it is due back, so he can borrow it. This policy is not perfect, since a patron can return the item before or after the time-stamp, but it is an indicator to the second borrower of when the item could become available. The last policy concerns overdue fines. Galvin Library has a policy of not pursuing overdue fines on its items, instead opting to invest staff time in unreturned books which are assumed lost. We consider the overdue fines that generate on an item automatically through the circulation system to be preventive and an opportunity to explain policy, rather than punitive. The library also views small fines that accrue as a possible wedge that can be created between the library, a unit of the university, and its relationship with future alumni.

In 2011 the annual Student Gift, which consists of funds collected by a committee of graduating students who work under the guidance of Institutional Advancement, awarded that year's monies to the library to be dedicated to the purchase of textbooks for the collection. The Student Gift committee would develop a list of projects on campus and then issue a survey of three options for students to vote on. In 2011 the textbook collection was the overwhelming choice, and the library received just under $20,000 to apply towards purchasing new textbooks. Somewhat ironically, students from that campaign described that gift as "completing the textbook collection" without realizing that it barely covered purchases for one year, with additional

FISCAL YEAR	TEXTBOOKS PURCHASED
2009 – 2010	417
2010 – 2011	312
2011 – 2012	230
2013 – 2014	170
2014 – 2015	101

Figure 5.1 | **Textbook Acquisitions by Fiscal Year: 2009–2014**

purchases necessary in succeeding years. One fact is that the acquisition of new textbooks decreases annually, as evidenced by the data shown in figure 5.1.

So the students are happier patrons, statistics for acquisition have steadily decreased, and use of the library has steadily increased. Based on circulation statistics of the reserve collection which have steadily increased, we can articulate that gate counts for library use that show increases of 3–6 percent annually over the last decade can be attributed to the use of the textbook collection.

The collection is currently made up of about 3,000 titles. If a textbook is not actively being used during a semester, it is kept on reserve and placed in a closed stacks area that is located near the circulation desk for easiest access. Previous editions of textbooks can be kept in both the active collection, depending on demand, or in closed stacks. The closed stacks' reserves items still circulate, but they are not returned to the circulating collection, which has different lending policies than reserves. For example, the loan period for the active reserves and closed stacks reserves is two hours, library use only, with an opportunity to renew for another two-hour time period, while the circulating collection has a lending period of a minimum of three weeks. The active reserves' collection circulates approximately 900 titles per semester, with an average annual circulation count in 2013–14 of just over 16,000. (See figure 5.2.)

Some study has been done on the 2012–13 fiscal year to try and determine why there was such a drop in circulation that school year, but no satisfying answers have been found to explain the drop.

The undergraduate textbook collection has also been used in the recruitment

FISCAL YEAR	NUMBER OF CHECKOUTS
2008 – 2009	6,936
2009 – 2010	11,157
2010 – 2011	17,997
2011 – 2012	17,925
2012 – 2013	11,689
2013 – 2014	16,219

Figure 5.2 | **Textbook Checkouts by Fiscal Year: 2009–2014**

of prospective students. Mentioned on tours given to future students who are visiting campus, it has become a unique resource that draws attention by students and parents alike when considering Illinois Tech as their future school. This recruitment action may be one of the underlying reasons for the original seed money given by a department connected to admissions.

Along with the positives that have resulted from starting an undergraduate textbook collection, there have been some negatives. Students would like more copies of each textbook purchased, but financial constraints allow for multiple copies only for large sections of more than sixty students. Every year students will petition the department, and sometimes the dean of libraries, to change the library use-only policy, or to purchase more copies. There is also a measure of unhappiness from graduate students because we do not have a dedicated textbook collection for their use. We do pull from circulation any titles that are being used as textbooks and place them on reserve, but the titles used in graduate classes are of a very different, and more specific, research type than undergraduate textbooks. This characteristic makes graduate textbooks less useful to a wide group of patrons, and therefore less collectible for broad use.

However, there is another obvious downside to the collection: sustainability. As demand has risen, it is the library's budget that has had to keep pace because there is no university, departmental, or donor support. Some liaisons, reserves collection staff, and administrative staff in public services and scholarly communications have started conversations with the faculty, asking them to consider not assigning a new edition of basic textbooks in the sciences, mathematics, and other topics every year. Furthermore, given the high prices of STEM textbooks, which can lead to students sharing or not purchasing textbooks at all, we know that students without access to assigned course materials can be left at a disadvantage. That's why we think this is a service worth continuing, and we are seeking answers to the sustainability issue.

DISCOVERING THE TEXTBOOK COLLECTION

Once purchasing and processing the items to create the reserve textbook collection was solved, the next hurdle was finding a solution so that students could easily locate those items. All of the books were available through our catalog, but there were difficulties in distinguishing textbooks from other library materials.

One problem area had to do with the catalog itself. Galvin Library is a member of the Consortium of Academic and Research Libraries in Illinois

(CARLI). This is an association of—at present—eighty-four member institutions whose goal is "to create and sustain a rich, supportive, and diverse knowledge environment that furthers teaching, learning, and research through the sharing of collections, expertise, and programs" ("CARLI Membership" 2016).

Governing members of CARLI can also petition to be included in I-Share, the consortium's merged union catalog. Participation in I-Share allows current students, faculty, and staff of member institutions to request physical materials from the union catalog and have them delivered to their local or another participating institution. They can also visit member institutions to borrow materials directly. These are benefits that Galvin Library has enjoyed since becoming both a CARLI and I-Share member in 1980 ("Illinois Institute of Technology" 2016).

General introductory textbooks often have very generic titles—such as *Biochemistry*, or *Introduction to Computer Programming*. If a student doesn't know the exact title, or if it was mistyped in the syllabus, the item record will not be displayed. The I-Share system that has been in use since the start of the collection is Ex Libris's Voyager ILS. CARLI originally implemented the Webvoyage catalog, and later included the VuFind front end as well. Both systems lack a recommender service that would highlight discrepancies in existing versus searched titles: for example, "Did you mean?" We explored using the reserves module in Voyager to manage the textbook collection, but found that it took too long to process the books in a timely manner. We did not have the expertise in-house to create a custom front end, and the nature of the union catalog allowed for few local customizations that would have assisted our efforts.

The reserves specialist at Galvin developed a workaround for the discovery problem. He created a Microsoft Access database to keep track of each semester's reserves. This did not include a front-end interface for students to use; circulation staff and student workers looked up items for the students on request. A new library website development effort started around this time, so the reserves system was incorporated into that effort. The new website was constructed using hand-coded pages in the PHP programming language, queried against a MySQL database. The digital services librarian at the time incorporated the Access table structure into the new site. He also developed a lookup system that students could use. It determined what semester was in session (fall, spring, or summer), and then generated a list of courses that could be selected to display the corresponding textbook(s). (See figure 5.3.) This system became available in about 2007.

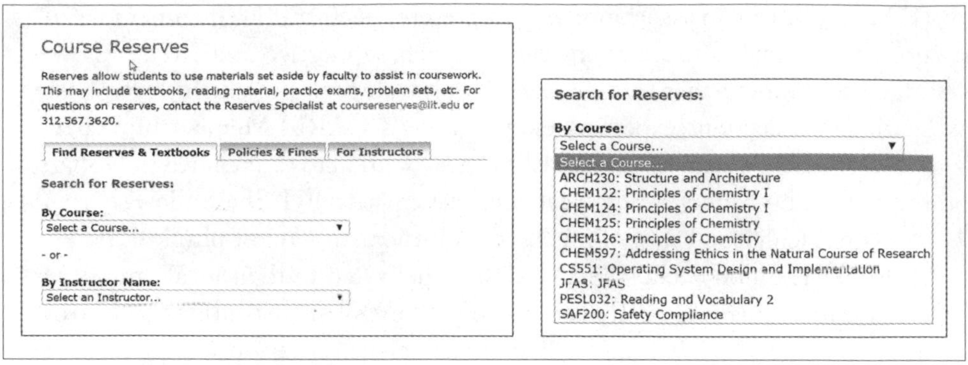

Figure 5.3 | **Course List with Textbooks**

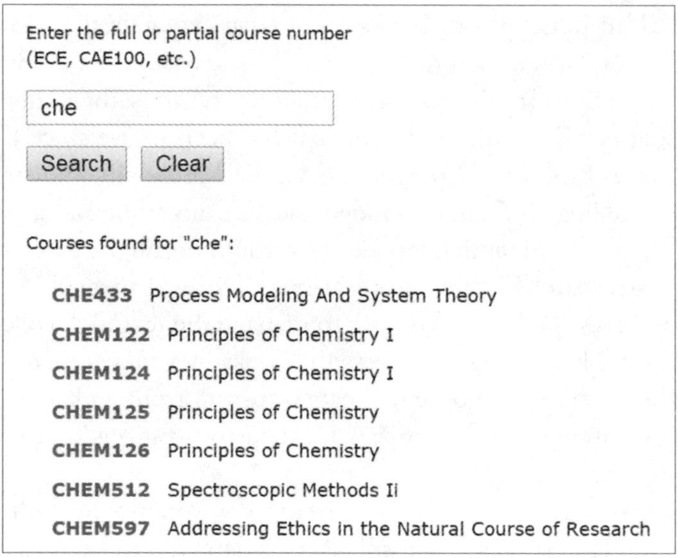

Figure 5.4 | **Search Results as Query Is Typed**

Several years later (2011), the new digital services librarian modified the lookup system to use AJAX (Asynchronous Javascript) technology. This allowed students to begin typing a course number and have search results appear as they typed (see figure 5.4) rather than using a long drop-down list.

This development effort was undertaken because the code would be reused for a new mobile website offered by Galvin. The mobile website was a site that was independent from the main library website, and only contained a small subset of information from the main site. The textbook lookup was one of the first items slated to appear on the mobile site (see figure 5.5) due to its popularity.

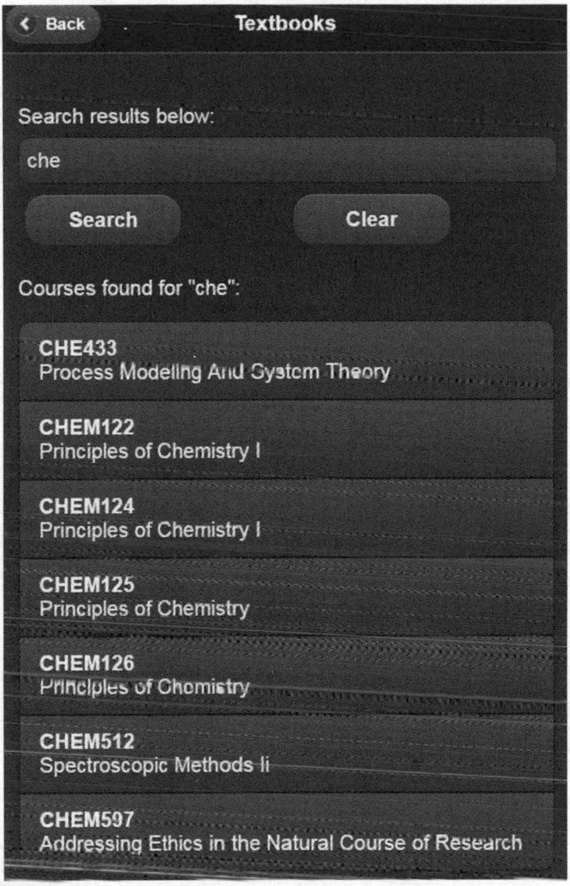

Figure 5.5 | **Textbook Lookup on Mobile Site**

The students now had a way to look up textbooks, but there were several problems with the system on the back end. First, the database table structure was ill-defined. A single table was used that included fields for textbook information along with course information (see figure 5.6). This meant that when multiple courses used the same textbook—or there were multiple sections of a course using the same book—multiple rows had to be entered into the database with the same textbook information. This made the process very prone to errors since all entries were entered by hand. There was no error-checking in place, so when a record didn't appear on the public lookup page, another record was added so that it would be displayed. The only way to edit a record once it was entered was to use the database administration interface; only the reserves specialist had access to this for security reasons. This made for many

| | Browse | Structure | SQL | Search | Insert | Export | Import | Operations | ▼ More |

#	Column	Type	Collation	Attributes	Null	Default	Extra	Action
1	reserve_item_id	mediumint(8)		UNSIGNED	No	None	AUTO_INCREMENT	Change Drop More ▼
2	active	enum('yes', 'no')	utf8_bin		No	no		Change Drop More ▼
3	reserve_type	enum('e-reserve', 'shelf')	utf8_bin		No	None		Change Drop More ▼
4	reserve_period	enum('fall', 'spring', 'summer', 'full year', 'per	utf8_bin		No	None		Change Drop More ▼
5	course_number	varchar(15)	utf8_bin		No	None		Change Drop More ▼
6	section	varchar(5)	utf8_bin		Yes	NULL		Change Drop More ▼
7	course_name	varchar(150)	utf8_bin		Yes	NULL		Change Drop More ▼
8	department	varchar(20)	utf8_bin		Yes	NULL		Change Drop More ▼
9	instructor_first_name	varchar(30)	utf8_bin		Yes	NULL		Change Drop More ▼
10	instructor_last_name	varchar(40)	utf8_bin		Yes	NULL		Change Drop More ▼
11	instructor_email	varchar(60)	utf8_bin		Yes	NULL		Change Drop More ▼
12	instructor_phone	varchar(18)	utf8_bin		Yes	NULL		Change Drop More ▼
13	doc_type	enum('article', 'book', 'book chapter', 'class mat	utf8_bin		No	None		Change Drop More ▼
14	file_name	varchar(100)	utf8_bin		Yes	NULL		Change Drop More ▼
15	doc_title	varchar(200)	utf8_bin		Yes	NULL		Change Drop More ▼
16	author	varchar(100)	utf8_bin		Yes	NULL		Change Drop More ▼
17	call_no	varchar(50)	utf8_bin		Yes	NULL		Change Drop More ▼
18	opac_url	varchar(200)	utf8_bin		Yes	NULL		Change Drop More ▼
19	loan_period	enum('2-hr', '4-hr', '24-hr', '3-day')	utf8_bin		Yes	NULL		Change Drop More ▼
20	notes	mediumtext	utf8_bin		Yes	NULL		Change Drop More ▼
21	post_date	datetime			No	None		Change Drop More ▼

Figure 5.6 | Textbook and Course Database Table

near-duplicate entries as students reentered information for an item whose record they could not edit. There were also many fields in the table structure that went unused, such as the professor's contact information and department.

When the textbook project first started, the process relied on receiving both the textbook and course information from the university bookstore. The bookstore manager would

1. Generate a report of textbook titles
2. Add the corresponding course numbers
3. Save the file in an Excel spreadsheet
4. Send the file to library staff

The reserves specialist would then make several modifications to the file. First he would add the missing information about the course, such as the course name, professor, and section number. Then he would fill in any missing or incorrect book information. Book edits most often included entering the full title name rather than the vendor system's abbreviated title. For example, the title *Vector Mechanics for Engineers: Statics* would display on the original list as VECTOR MECH . . . , STATICS.

Eventually, adding the course information to the textbook report became too time-consuming for the bookstore manager. He switched to using the original report format. This format included the same truncated book information as above, but only included an internal record ID for the related course, meaning that the course name, number, section, and professor would have to be added by hand. The reserves specialist and his students would look up this additional information as well and add it to the spreadsheet, as well as the URL to the holdings record for books that were already in the collection. After all of the data manipulation was complete, the list was ready and the records were manually added to the database.

The digital services librarian began batch-loading entries into the system to reduce the work of entering records by hand. However, this could only happen after the reserves staff had manually updated the incorrect or missing information, which took a considerable amount of time. Several macro scripts were run in order to clean the data so that it could be batch-uploaded into the database. The batch upload reduced the workload, but there was still the arduous task of manually looking up the complete book information beforehand. The process took several days to complete from start to finish. It would also have to be repeated at least twice each semester to pick up any late additions of textbooks from faculty. By the time all of the titles were received, edited, and imported into the database, it was often several weeks into the semester.

In 2014 a major website revision was started. The Drupal content management system (CMS) was selected because this was the system the university chose for its new website, which had been launched the previous year. Drupal can easily be extended from the basic installation of its core code by using "modules": additional functionality written by the open source community and offered for reuse (Tomlinson 2010). The new website was launched in August 2015 for the start of the fall semester. The old site was kept running and switched to another domain because it still hosted some processes that had not yet been ported over—the textbook lookup page being one of them. Having overcome the learning curve of working with Drupal for the initial launch of the site, we were comfortable enough with the new system to tackle reimagining the textbook process from both the public and staff perspective.

The first step in rethinking the process was meeting with the library staff involved in the purchasing and processing of textbooks. This included the reserves specialist, whose position manages textbooks and other reserve items (such as videos and instructor copies) as well as group study rooms. Representatives from the Technical Services Department and the digital services librarian were also involved. We talked through the process; one problem that was discussed was the limited amount of course information that was included in the report. Also, it was delivered via e-mail as an Excel spreadsheet, but there were often formatting issues that had to be corrected. This led to a trip to the on-campus bookstore to meet with the manager. The bookstore uses a closed system from a private vendor to coordinate textbook purchases—one we don't have access to. A brief investigation into the options of this system uncovered an additional export option that was much simpler for all parties: a fixed-width text report. This simple format required no additional formatting by the bookstore manager. There was less data involved than in the previous version, but it contained the crucial combination of ISBN and course ID that was needed. Course information details, we discovered, can be downloaded directly in spreadsheet form from Illinois Tech's internal system for each semester. These were easily uploaded into the Drupal CMS. Drupal allows users to create custom record types, known as "content types." These content types are a default set of values and constraints ("Content Types" 2016) for the data designated as that type of record. We created a content type of "Course" to store this information. This was completed with little additional effort from the team.

The digital services librarian had written a program for another project that retrieved bibliographic data by ISBN from the WorldCat Search API from OCLC. This was done to retrieve descriptions for our leisure reading collection from the MARC21 520 field of the OCLC bibliographic record. Since the bulk of the work was already completed, she was able to adapt the script to use with the textbook collection. This removed the burden of looking up the complete title information for each textbook by the reserves staff. The script runs quickly—it generally takes less than two minutes to retrieve information for the 200–300 unique titles used in a given semester. An additional content type of "Textbook" was created in Drupal to store this data, and included a relationship with the Course content type. Multiple courses could now be attached to a single textbook record. This allowed for the crucial one-to-many record relationship that our previous system had lacked.

The Views module for Drupal allowed us to create the public lookup interface without having to write any custom code. This module allows users to create custom queries, filters, and sorting for records of one or more content types; one can also expose these settings so that they can be used in a public interface. This functionality allowed us to focus on designing a more useful textbook lookup tool for students. We were able to construct a search function that students could use to search by any number of criteria: course number, name, professor, book title, and so on (see figure 5.7).

The next step in the process was rethinking the work of the reserves staff. The Drupal CMS allowed us to build an internal interface so that textbooks and courses could be easily viewed and modified. The reserves specialist and his student workers needed an interface that displayed the information in a format they needed, and also allowed records to be added, modified, or deleted. Again, we used the Views module to create several custom reports. Not needing to schedule additional time for a separate development effort allowed us to focus on the needs of our internal users instead: the reserves specialist and his student workers. The digital services librarian interviewed the reserves specialist about his workflow and what types of information would be best for him to see on a single-screen report. The report was built on a test server that mirrored the production environment. For the fall 2015 semester, the reserves specialist worked with the current production system, and would occasionally switch over to the test system to perform the same task. This allowed him to highlight the kinds of problems he had with the current system, as well as make suggestions for the new system. After a few changes, the report below was the one that went live for the spring 2016 semester (see figure 5.8).

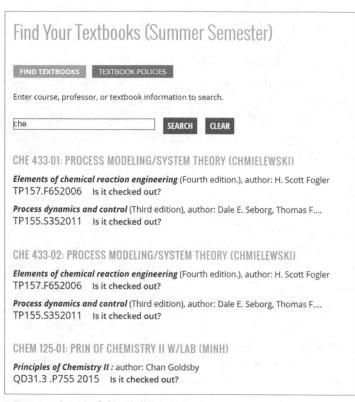

Figure 5.7 | **Search by Various Criteria**

Because we now had a system that allowed us to easily build queries and reports without the need for a professional database administrator, we were able to generate additional reports that used to be created by hand, including a list of call numbers for the upcoming semester that students would use to fetch titles for shifting, a list of textbooks that needed to be ordered by the technical services staff, and a list of books that were already on order and awaiting receipt.

Reserves staff would also need to add new textbooks to the system (to accommodate professors' personal items and late entries). Adding and editing records in a CMS is not an issue, but ensuring that the data was formatted correctly was a problem. Using the Rules module in Drupal, we were able to enforce a few constraints. First, that the record numbers that identify a specific course and section (CRN) could not be changed; these numbers are generated by the university system and are static, so there is no reason they would need to be modified once they were input into the system.

Enter any textbook, professor, or course information to search.
All textbook records will display. Course information will display only if the CRN is linked in the textbook record.

1467 items found

Semester
[- Any - ▼]

(Search) (Clear)

COURSE CRN	PUBLISHED? (COURSE)	COURSE NUMBER (FULL)	COURSE NAME	PROFESSOR	ISBN	PUBLISHED? (TEXTBOOK)	BOOK TITLE	EDITION	AUTHOR	CALL NUMBER	ORDER STATUS	LINKED CATALOG RECORD?	SEMESTER	POST DATE
28199	No Edit course	SSCI 480-01	Intro to Survey Methodology	Emmons	9780470465482	No Edit textbook	Survey methodology	2nd ed.	Robert M. Groves, Floyd J. Fowler, Jr. Mick P. Couuper, James M. Lepkowski, Eleanor Singer	HA31.2 .S783 2009		Yes		Monday, December 21, 2015 - 15.44
19195	Yes Edit course	SSCI 323-91	Problems of Multi-Ethnic Relig	Ireland	9780205742201	Yes Edit textbook	Understanding ethnic conflict :	4th ed.	Raymond Taras, Rajat Ganguly	GN496.T372010		Yes	Fall	Monday, July 11, 2016 - 16.50
28196	No Edit course	SSCI 319-01	Comparative Health Systems	Ireland	9781137023568	No Edit textbook	Comparative health policy	Fourth edition.	Robert H. Blank and Viola Burau	RA394 .B56 2014		Yes		Monday, December 21, 2015 - 15.45
19194	Yes Edit course	SSCI 318-01	Global Health	Ireland	9781284018547	Yes Edit textbook	Global health 101	2nd edition.	Richard Skolnik	RA441 .S56 2012	Need to Order	Yes	Fall	Monday, July 11, 2016 - 16.50
33102	Yes Edit course	SSCI 313-01	Global Health	Ireland	9780763829755	Yes Edit textbook	Global health 101	2nd ed.	Richard Skolnik	RA441 .S56 2012		Yes	Summer	Thursday, May 26, 2016 - 11.41
28195	No Edit course	SSCI 225-01	Geographic Information Systems	Huang	9781118676950	No Edit textbook	Geographic information science & systems	Fourth edition.	Paul A. Longley, University College London, UK, Michael F. Goodchild, ...	G70.212 .L658 2015		Yes		Monday, November 16, 2015 - 11.45

Figure 5.8 | **Report for Reserves Staff**

The next two rules concerned the ISBN field. First, we had to ensure that students only input numbers for the ISBN and didn't include any dashes. This is because our OPAC will return a "not found" message if a search is done with an ISBN that contains dashes. The textbook report delivered by the bookstore does contain dashes, but our API script removes them. Adding a rule that only allows numbers in the field ensures that this format is kept. The second constraint on the textbook record type ensured that the ISBN field remained unique. This was a common problem with the old system: multiple entries were added so that each course using the book would be included in a search. Even multiple entries for the same book and course combination were entered in error. In the new system, when a textbook record is added manually with an ISBN field that already exists in the database, the record is not saved, an error message is displayed onscreen, and a link to the original record is provided so that the user can perform the necessary update.

CONCLUSION

The library staff will continue to review the policies and procedures that comprise our textbook collection as our needs and budgets continue to change. We look forward to investigating other alternatives to textbooks, such as partnering with faculty to provide open educational resources. We also would like an opportunity to find a donor to endow such a collection to improve the financial sustainability of a resource that is so valuable to student success. Until then, Galvin Library has committed to continuing the textbook collection as a way to alleviate this particular obstacle and financially stressful component of being a student.

Bibliography

"CARLI Membership Agreement | CARLI." 2016. https://www.carli.illinois.edu/membership/memagree.

"Content Types | Drupal.org." 2016. https://www.drupal.org/node/21947.

"Illinois Institute of Technology | CARLI." 2016. https://www.carli.illinois.edu/mem-libs/mem-inst?member_id=41.

Tomlinson, Todd. *Beginning Drupal 7.* New York: Apress, 2010. http://link.springer.com/book/10.1007%2F978-1-4302-2860-8.

6

EVOLUTION OF A TEXTBOOK CIRCULATION PROGRAM

Outcomes of Demand-Driven versus Strategic Selection Policies

Posie Aagaard and Jan H. Kemp

What involvement do academic librarians have—or should they have—in supporting textbooks? The issue of whether or how to provide access to textbooks has generated considerable discussion—and little agreement— among academic librarians over the years. Providing print textbooks for every student in every class has been beyond the budget, space, and service capacities of most libraries. Although some libraries decided there was no role for the library in providing access to textbooks in the print environment, others developed programs to address the demand for textbook lending to one degree or another.[1]

This chapter discusses the genesis and evolution of a successful textbook lending program at the University of Texas at San Antonio (UTSA), tracing its growth from a small, unfunded service to a robust program that accounted for 50 percent of the libraries' circulation of physical materials in the fiscal year 2015. Initially, we did not purchase textbooks, and only textbooks provided by faculty or requested by faculty were available on reserve. However, in 2009 librarians changed the textbook policy and began selecting textbooks to support high-enrollment classes for freshman and sophomore students—those who represent the greatest retention risk at our university. Several years later, a patron-driven textbook acquisitions (PDA) approach was adopted in combination with the textbook purchases for lower-division classes.

Although the PDA purchases increased textbook circulation, they also resulted in much higher textbook expenditures, and we found ourselves purchasing many textbooks for low-enrollment, upper-division and graduate classes. As a public university with 30,000 students, librarians thought it was important to use the limited textbook allocation to support the university goals of increasing student retention and graduation rates. Lending textbooks to support the lower-division, high-enrollment classes had the potential to support student success on a larger scale.

More recently, the libraries textbook program has expanded to include identifying and purchasing textbooks available in electronic format, and helping to foster the adoption of low or no-cost textbooks on campus as part of a nascent open educational resources initiative. After six years of growth, textbook lending has become an increasingly popular and valued service—one that will continue to evolve as the textbook landscape changes. Over time, textbooks in electronic format and OERs will likely reduce the demand for a physical textbook lending service. During the transition, the UTSA Libraries' strategies and outcomes may prove useful for libraries investigating different options and approaches for lending textbooks.

INSTITUTIONAL CONTEXT

The University of Texas at San Antonio, founded in 1969, is the third largest of fourteen universities in the University of Texas system. UTSA enrolls 30,000 students, and from 2000 to 2010 it was one of the fastest-growing universities in Texas with a growth rate of 39 percent over the previous decade. The university offers 63 bachelor programs, 51 master programs, and 24 doctoral programs. UTSA is designated as a Hispanic Serving Institution, and Hispanic students make up just over 50 percent of the student body. More than 60 percent of students are identified as minorities, and in 2014, 47 percent were first-generation college students, and nearly that many were economically disadvantaged or eligible for federal Pell grants. The university offers a number of academic support programs, and several of these are located in the library: the Q-Lab, providing peer tutoring in quantitative subjects; Supplemental Instruction, a program that organizes peer-led weekly tutoring sessions for classes with low student success rates; PIVOT, a grant-funded program to support first-generation students; and the Writing Center. Given the institutional context and the libraries' experience with the high circulation of faculty-owned textbooks on reserves, we thought that any textbook support we offered could be beneficial.

ORIGIN OF THE TEXTBOOK PURCHASING PROGRAM

In summer 2009 the libraries had a relatively small collection of textbooks on reserve, composed largely of copies instructors had placed on reserve for their classes. The textbooks were heavily used by students, and as the fall 2009 semester approached it was clear that many of the textbooks could not withstand another semester of use. Many were falling apart, and the parts were literally held together with rubber bands. These items had circulated far more often than any other type of physical material the library owned, yet our existing collection development policies did not include an allocation for textbook purchases. If subject librarians wished, they could request a copy of a textbook and place it on reserve for a certain class or add it to the general collection; however, these items were purchased with the librarian's firm order funds. Similarly, if an instructor requested that a textbook be purchased and placed on reserve, the request would be routed to the subject librarian who would decide whether to use the firm order allocation to purchase the item. There was no collections fund to replace the heavily circulated textbooks, nor did interlibrary loan policies allow students to request current textbooks.

Since we could not continue to circulate the worn out textbook copies, librarians decided to recommend changing the collections policy and request collections funds to replace the worn-out textbooks. The decision was not made lightly, because allocating funds for textbooks would mean lower allocations for firm orders. However, the high circulation figures for our existing textbooks provided sufficient justification for an initial $15,000 for a pilot project.

TEXTBOOK PILOT PROJECT

A textbook project plan was developed in fall 2009 by a team led by the heads of the Access Services and Acquisitions departments. The goal was to develop and implement selection and ordering procedures and have the additional textbooks available at the start of the spring 2010 semester. Working within the constraints of this small allocation, Access Services identified the freshman and sophomore-level courses with the highest enrollments. These courses were identified by requesting a course enrollment report for all lower-division classes and then sorting the courses from highest to lowest enrollments. We began with courses that had the highest enrollments and went down the list of courses, identifying those with textbooks that cost more than $100. We did not identify an enrollment threshold for which to purchase books, since budget constraints limited textbook purchasing to a relatively small number of courses.

After determining the cost of the textbooks for each course, we selected 110 textbooks for high-enrollment classes that had expensive textbooks. We believed these criteria would provide the greatest advantage to those students who were most in need of academic support. After setting up an account with the campus bookstore, we purchased textbooks in a range of subject areas including math, biology, chemistry, English, psychology, business, and history, among others.

The program required close coordination between the Access Services Department, which selected the textbooks, and the Acquisitions Department, which ordered the materials. It was important to have the new textbooks available prior to the start of classes, because students normally checked to see if we owned their textbooks within the first week of class. If a textbook was unavailable when the student initially checked, the student would not usually return to check again later. A 2011 article provides additional details about this process (Chang and Garrison).[2]

The addition of high-demand textbooks on two-hour reserve increased the number of transactions at the front desk, and hourly circulation figures were studied to ensure that the desk was adequately staffed to handle demand at peak times. Due to the heavy demand for textbooks, the Access Services Department began maintaining a waiting list for textbooks and purchased a pager system similar to those used in restaurants. If a textbook was checked out, the student's name was placed on the waiting list, and he or she was given a pager. When the textbook became available, the student was notified via the pager.

ONGOING ALLOCATIONS FOR TEXTBOOKS

The increased circulation following purchase of the additional textbooks had clearly justified the allocation of collections funds, and this allocation became an ongoing, if modest, component of the materials budget. Lists of textbooks for purchase were manually prepared twice each year prior to the fall and spring semesters by the Access Services Department on the main campus, and by the head of the downtown campus library. Access Services staff manually searched the bookstore's online textbook database to identify the cost of textbooks for high-enrollment classes. The selection criteria continued to emphasize lower-division, high-enrollment classes with expensive textbooks. The price floor was loosely set at $100; however, some less expensive textbooks were also purchased when large numbers of students requested the textbook.

The allocation also provided a source of funds for lower-division textbooks requested by faculty or subject librarians, relieving librarians of the need to purchase these textbooks with firm order funds. In general, upper-division and graduate-level textbooks continued to be ordered with the subject librarians' firm order funds, provided that funds were available. In addition, if Access Services received multiple student requests for a textbook, the item was often selected for purchase. Multiple copies—sometimes as many as six—were purchased for those textbooks in the highest demand. Decisions about ordering multiple copies were made by reviewing the waiting lists to see which textbooks appeared most frequently.

After the initial expenditure of $15,000 in FY 2010, textbook expenditures averaged approximately $23,000 per year from 2011 to 2014. This expenditure figure does not include the cost of the upper-division and graduate textbooks the subject librarians purchased from firm order funds. This relatively small textbook allocation allowed the library to purchase replacement copies for worn-out textbooks, buy new editions of heavily used textbooks, and add some new textbook titles. During this time the average cost of textbooks increased, which meant that fewer textbooks could be added, given a textbook allocation that did not increase appreciably.

GROWTH OF TEXTBOOK CIRCULATION

It has become axiomatic that the circulation of physical materials in academic libraries has declined as the availability of high-quality content in digital format has increased. This trend was not seen with the circulation of reserves materials after the new textbooks were made available. On the contrary, in one year, from fiscal year 2011 (September 2010-August 2011) to fiscal year 2012 (September 2011-August 2012), reserves circulation increased by

FY13	TOTAL (%)	FY14	TOTAL (%)	FY15	TOTAL (%)
55,532	32.6	64,180	39.5	83,688	50.0

Figure 6.1 | **Textbook Circulations**

FY13	TOTAL (%)	FY14	TOTAL (%)	FY15	TOTAL (%)
114,779	67.4	98,285	60.5	83,561	50.0

Figure 6.2 | **General Collection Circulations**

24 percent. During the same period, the circulation of physical materials in the general collection declined by 14 percent. Unfortunately, we had no way to determine the exact number of textbook circulations, because textbooks were not identified as a material type separate from the other books in the reserves collection. In August 2012, to provide more accurate statistics on textbook usage, we created a new material type for textbooks and updated the records of current textbooks on reserve with the textbook designation. Procedures were also changed to ensure that future textbooks added to the collection would be assigned the textbook material type. Due to this change, since 2012 we have been able to more accurately track the circulation of textbooks.

In the period since we added the textbook material type, we have seen a 51 percent increase in the circulation of textbooks. The chart in figure 6.1 shows the textbook circulation over the past three fiscal years.

During the same period, the circulation of physical materials in the library's general collection declined by 27 percent. Comparing the circulation of textbooks with the circulation of items in the general collection (see figure 6.2) shows that our textbook expenditures, a small segment of the budget for print materials, is responsible for an increasing percentage of print circulation.

MARKETING

In collaboration with the library's Communications Department, Public Services librarians added textbook lending to its list of principal services. We marketed textbook lending via oversized posters in library elevators, in library brochures, on the website, in the orientation video shown to incoming freshmen, and via social media. We wanted all students, particularly students who were new to campus, to be aware of the service. However, while our collection of textbooks was growing each year, it only provided books for a relatively small number of courses. The marketing materials let students know we provided textbooks on reserve, but in retrospect, the enthusiastic tone of our marketing may have somewhat over-promised the availability of textbooks, since many students would find out that we had only one of their books, and often we had none of them.

After a couple of years of marketing the textbook lending service, we realized that some students were beginning to expect—and even demand—that we provide all of their textbooks. It was necessary to change the wording of our marketing to emphasize that we carry only a selection of textbooks. Further, we realized that some students assumed that having the textbook on reserve would be adequate to meet their academic needs. In reality, with the large enrollments in some classes, getting access to the textbook could be frustrating. So, a word to the wise: do not over-promise! In recent semesters, during the first week of class, we offered a textbook information service point near the circulation desk that was staffed by the libraries' peer research coaches. These well-trained student workers offered to help students check to see if we owned their textbooks, and taught students how to determine whether their textbooks were available on reserve.

RESULTS FROM THE FIRST FOUR YEARS

As noted previously, the increase in the number of textbooks boosted reserves circulation, increasing activity at the service desk. Students greatly appreciated having access to their textbooks, and through messages on comment cards, via online comments, and in LibQUAL survey ratings and comments, students expressed a high level of satisfaction with textbook lending. A related challenge for both students and staff, however, was the fact that the Voyager ILS reserves system did not allow users to search by title, which complicated the search process. As a result, many students came to the desk to ask whether their textbooks were available, which challenged the principle of enabling students to be self-sufficient users of the library. On the positive side, checking for textbook availability gave staff the opportunity to interact with students more often, making the students feel welcome and incidentally informing them about other services. For example, a review of circulation statistics showed that it was common for students to check out a laptop at the same time they checked out a textbook.

Undoubtedly, the increased use of textbooks also contributed to increased gate counts. For the past several years, at busy times during the fall semester, over 9,000 individuals have used the John Peace Library on a daily basis—a figure that equals nearly one-third of the UTSA student body.

The textbook service also raised a valid concern among librarians that students might think they did not need to own a copy of their textbook if the book was available on reserve. Depending on access to a textbook on reserve could cause problems when many students needed access to a textbook at the same time. Some students were on the waiting list for as much as four hours or more before a book became available. Clearly, this reliance on such a limited resource was not optimal for academic success. It also placed additional stress on the staff who were trying to assist the frustrated students. Despite these challenges, by and large students greatly appreciated the service and used it heavily.

THE GET IT FOR ME SERVICE

The libraries embarked on a project to streamline requests for all types of materials, regardless of whether they were owned or not owned. The goal of the project was to give users a one-stop, simplified means to request the items they needed. The theory was that users should not need to know whether an item was owned, held at a remote location, or eligible for interlibrary loan. The service was branded "Get It For Me" (GIFM). GIFM pre-populates ILLiad request forms with bibliographic information from library online resources, such as our "QuickSearch" discovery service or the online catalog, and streamlines the routing and processing of requests. The GIFM service was immediately popular with users.

A NEW APPROACH: INCORPORATING DEMAND-DRIVEN TEXTBOOKS

In early 2013, an assessment of the interlibrary loan service showed that a considerable number of ILL requests were unfilled. In an effort to reduce the number of requests for items too new or scarce to borrow from other libraries, we began purchasing these items on demand. ILL staff reviewed the queue of unfilled requests and purchased titles that matched cost, subject area, and other criteria developed with the subject librarians.

The growing student demand for textbooks observed at our reserves desks was soon echoed in an increasing number of unfilled ILL requests for textbooks. Meanwhile, the libraries' ITHAKA S&R local faculty survey revealed that our faculty rely heavily on textbooks for student research assignments. Collectively, these indicators led the library to expand on-demand purchasing to include textbooks. To provide equitable access, we implemented a policy to place all items identified as textbooks on two-hour reserve.

If students expressed concern that their textbook was not available, public services staff could inform them that they could request the textbook through GIFM. The ease with which textbooks could be requested through GIFM created a "perfect storm" of orders. New textbooks began flooding the reserves shelves, which quickly became crowded. The on-demand textbook program's instant popularity and subsequent sharp increase in expenditures made it abundantly clear that we needed to establish purchasing parameters, so we worked with subject librarians to create broad guidelines. There were no textbook purchasing exclusions by course level; even graduate-level textbooks were purchased.

As in the past, if we owned a requested title electronically, we would refer the user to the electronic version rather than purchasing a copy in print. At this point, relatively few e-textbooks were available for purchase by libraries. However, if the textbook was available on a user-friendly platform with multiple simultaneous users, the e-format was preferred for purchasing, as it was (and still is) in most of our collection development areas.

We continued to purchase print textbooks for high-enrollment, lower-level courses with expensive textbooks, as well as textbooks requested by librarians on behalf of faculty, along with textbooks in the new on-demand program. New fund codes were created to more accurately track the varied textbook program costs and circulations, so we would be able to better assess the costs versus use for textbook purchases.

A CAUTIONARY TALE

Data from the expanded program revealed some important trends. Despite positive outcomes such as increased textbook circulation and much higher fill rates for the ILL service, a number of challenges had arisen. We were unable to readily identify adopted textbooks, which precipitated a suboptimal chain of events: (1) intensive ILL staff effort was required to identify and process textbook requests, particularly during periods of highest demand; (2) some textbooks were inadvertently routed to non-reserves locations and snapped up by enterprising students for longer checkout periods, and were often not returned to the libraries in a timely manner; and (3) other students easily discovered and requested the missing non-reserves-located textbooks through the GIFM service. Ultimately, this resulted in duplicated staff effort and expending of funds to purchase duplicate copies of textbooks that should have been unnecessary.

In addition, the on-demand model favored students who were familiar with the GIFM service, leading to a disproportionate number of textbook purchases for graduate students. Students' expectations of the textbook program quickly became inflated, leading some to demand that we purchase all adopted textbooks. Our print textbook program was never intended to supplant students' need to purchase their own textbook copies, but rather to supplement their access to the required materials. A comprehensive purchase of textbooks was not feasible for the libraries' budget. Moreover, we did not believe that it would best match our goal of ensuring that our limited resources support the academic success of our large body of freshman and sophomore students.

In FY 2015, overall textbook expenditures totaled over $75,000 as part of a total materials budget of $5,600,000. Although we carefully allocated, monitored, and adjusted textbook funds, we determined that a student on-demand textbook program was not the best use of scarce collections funds. Earlier this year, we began a project to redefine the textbook program and clarify its goals—including the main goal of supporting student success.

"THIRD TIME IS A CHARM"

Because our textbook service models evolved along different paths at different times, our methods for providing textbooks were inadvertently siloed into programs with distinctly different purposes that risked being at odds with each other. We brainstormed revised goals to refocus our efforts on supporting those students most at risk—primarily those in lower-division, large survey classes whose required textbooks are expensive. It is also important for us to continue to work with faculty who view our reserves service as crucial to the success of their courses. In order to best meet these goals, we consolidated textbook purchases for lower-division courses and faculty requests into a unified program, effectively eliminating the student demand-driven program.

To put these changes into effect, we mobilized a new multi-department project team led by our department heads for Metadata and Collection Support and Library Systems. We engaged individuals directly involved in various aspects of the work—including those in Access Services and Public Services, Cataloging, Library Systems, Acquisitions/ILL/ER, and Collections/Subject librarians—to review, update, and document new processes. Group members created a data flow diagram to illustrate the new process for retrieving and integrating textbook, course section, and enrollment data (figure 6.3). We also worked to create a space management strategy for the textbook collection, which is made possible by new processes for selecting and maintaining these materials.

PROCESS IMPROVEMENTS

We established new connections with other campus offices to receive never-before-seen data that now fully informs our goals for the revised textbook program by providing student retention and graduation data. The improvements span a wide range of areas.

For the first time ever, we have an authoritative list of adopted textbooks. It took time, persistence, and the help of campus colleagues for permission to screen scrape the campus bookstore's website for textbook information. The Library Systems Department created custom code to scrape the website's HTML into a local database. Just recently, we were granted permission to retrieve daily data files from the campus bookstore with additional data points, such as a textbook designation of "required" or "optional."

In addition, we receive data feeds from the Registrar's Office that provide course, section, instructor, and enrollment data, as well as feeds from the Office of Institutional Effectiveness detailing the number of students who earned grades of D or F or withdrew from a course. Our Library Systems team created programs to automatically identify the print and e-textbooks we already own that are included in the bookstore list of current textbooks; calculate average textbook costs per student and by department or college; identify various textbook assignment trends; and display enrollment figures, compiling enrollment for all sections of a class. These analyses are valuable not only to librarians and library administrators, but also to faculty and campus administrators.

At this early point in the new venture, the average cost of a textbook is approximately $200. We ordered several hundred titles, including an additional copy for every 100 students enrolled in a lower-division, high-impact course. We cap the number of copies purchased at five or six, due to space and budget constraints.

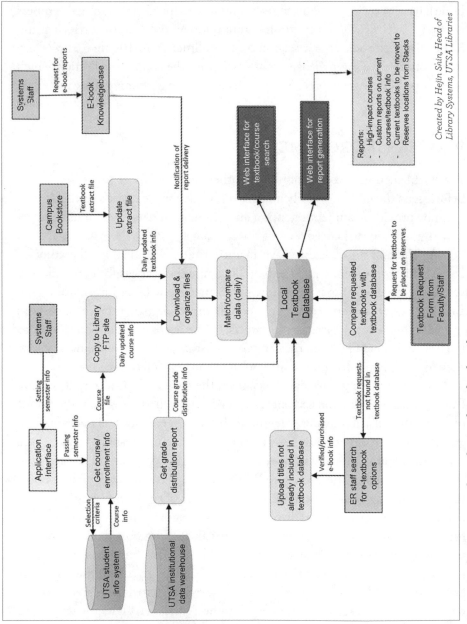

Created by Hejin Shin, Head of Library Systems, UTSA Libraries

Figure 6.3 | **Ingestion and Synthesis of Textbook and Course Data**

We use aggregated enrollment, grade, and textbook cost data to categorize courses as "high-impact." We then calculate the estimated costs to purchase one or more print textbook copies to support courses with the most critical need. For example, the first-semester freshman-level calculus course uses a textbook that costs $200. The class is considered "high-impact" because it is a core course for a number of majors, and also because a fairly high number of students earn grades of D or F, or withdraw from the class. Over 1,200 students are enrolled in the course, and we have purchased six copies of the book despite the high enrollment, since we generally cap the number of copies purchased for any course at six. We identify additional lower-priority tiers to support in the event that funding is available.

Holdings match reports allow us to identify books adopted as textbooks that reside in other non-reserves locations. Each semester, we review these and move adopted textbooks to the reserves shelves. This helps avoid the need to recall textbooks or purchase replacement copies to place on reserve.

Now that print and e-textbook holdings are automatically matched as the data streams are combined, we can dependably publicize our e-books as a viable textbook option. We add e-textbook titles and links to the course reserves system for ready identification by students, faculty, and staff alike. However, our electronic resources staff members check each e-book title before including it in the course reserves list of textbooks to ensure that the license allows at least three simultaneous users and the publisher platform meets basic usage requirements. We also rely on new semi-automated list-checking processes to identify textbooks available as e-books that we may be able to purchase. Limited simultaneous user access models are especially problematic for e-books that publishers and providers categorize as "textbooks"; such e-books are not generally purchased in lieu of print copies.

A simple database for staff integrates textbook selection and cost information, course/section/enrollment data, and local print and online holdings. Preprogrammed, live reports provide the analyses mentioned above. Librarians may request titles on behalf of faculty for which the libraries have no holdings; a new request form auto-populates a textbook's bibliographic information, which saves time and improves accuracy. A separate course reserves request form that resides on the libraries' public website relies on Shibboleth to restrict access only to faculty and staff, effectively excluding student requests. A regularly scheduled computer program that runs behind the scenes now automatically records these course reserves requests.

The project's scope did not include developing processes or systems to mimic or replace the functionality of a commercial course reserves system.

We are not currently considering such a system, although we expect that the project will potentially lead us to improve discovery solutions for textbooks. This will prepare us to incorporate new textbook access models such as OER and pay-per-view digital material course packs.

DISCUSSION AND CONCLUSION

The libraries employ a robust suite of demand-driven programs and routinely base collection decisions on use and cost data. Our collections support an aspiring tier one institution; we strive to balance needs for print and online materials in ways that are most cost-efficient and format-appropriate. Although some libraries' collection policies do not include textbooks, the high rate of print circulations for textbooks in our program reflects a compelling need and provides a solid justification for our institution to expend funds for textbook purchases. Considering the 51 percent increase in print textbook circulation from fiscal year 2013 to 2015, our relatively small expenditure for these textbooks seems to be an excellent value.

Our print textbook program is one piece of an overall textbook strategy. Physical copies are inherently limited in that each copy can only be used by one person at a time. Therefore, we proactively identify and pursue multiuser e-textbooks as a preferred access option, and we expect to purchase more textbooks electronically as they become available. We also lead the campus in the movement to incorporate OER materials into courses, providing faculty workshops and grants to raise awareness and support OER adoption. In the future—hopefully the near future—we expect the increased availability of textbooks in electronic format and OER together will reduce the demand for print textbooks on reserve. The data we are compiling will help to inform our discussions with faculty and campus leaders as we explore OER options to relieve the cost burden for students.

In the meantime, we will continue to offer this high-demand service. Although we cannot purchase all textbooks for all classes due to cost and space constraints, we will continue to purchase textbooks for selected lower-division, high-enrollment classes as one of our many initiatives to support student academic success. For our library, the textbook program is another way to demonstrate value.

Notes

1. Steven Bell, "Textbook Turmoil: The Library's Role in the Textbook Revolution," *Library Issues* 31 (2010): 1–4.
2. Amy Chang and Judy Garrison, "Textbook Lending Service: Providing a Service Students Need When They Need It," *College & Research Library News* 72, no. 9 (2011): 527–30, http://crln.acrl.org/content/72/9/527.full.

Bibliography

Bell, Steven. "Textbook Turmoil: The Library's Role in the Textbook Revolution." *Library Issues* 31 (2010): 1–4.

Chang, Amy, and Judy Garrison. "Textbook Lending Service: Providing a Service Students Need When They Need It." *College & Research Library News* 72, no. 9 (2011): 527–30. http://crln.acrl.org/content/72/9/527.full.

CAN HARD-COPY TEXTBOOKS ON LIBRARY RESERVE HELP ADDRESS THE TEXTBOOK DILEMMA?

Feng-Ru Sheu, Kay Downey, and Tom Klingler

Traditionally, academic libraries have not actively collected or purchased textbooks for their collections for the following reasons: (1) it is considered the students' responsibility to buy textbooks on their own; (2) it is impractical and unsustainable for academic libraries to pay for and house the innumerable volumes needed to support student textbook needs; (3) textbooks are frequently replaced by newer editions and do not provide long-term value to the library; and (4) many universities protect campus bookstores' revenue.[1]

But the rising cost of textbooks, compounded by the rapid succession of new editions and the increased requirement for multimedia textbooks, is a major concern in academia. Textbook affordability impacts many factors such as dropout rate, retention, and most importantly student learning.[2] Buczynski writes that some students do not purchase required textbooks because they are financially unable to do so or may not register for certain classes due to textbook affordability.[3] This creates inequality in the classroom and directly affects student success.

In recent years, academic libraries have offered print textbooks on reserve for students who cannot afford them. Today, as textbook costs become more difficult to manage, many academic libraries are reformulating their collection policies, taking into consideration textbook acquisitions and renewing their efforts in traditional library services such as course packs and reserves.[4] Reserve services for print textbooks exist in university libraries such as George Mason University, the University of Minnesota, Virginia Tech, and UCLA, to name a few.[5] George Mason University Libraries initiated their program after observing the disproportionate number of textbooks being requested via interlibrary loan. UCLA recognized the need and expanded their course reserves services for undergraduate courses to include textbooks.[6] Program details vary but fundamentally accomplish the same goal. By expanding the collection services to include materials most valuable to the user, the library can provide a much-needed service and help level the socioeconomic playing field.

The textbook reserve services do have drawbacks and have been criticized as ineffectual, primarily for the reason that students may be unable to rely on the textbook being available at the point of need, particularly during times of high demand, when deadlines and exams are looming. The services also face criticism as a weak panacea in the face of mounting concern over the high cost of course materials.[7] Although it is true that the textbooks on reserve service cannot be considered an all-encompassing solution to the textbook dilemma, providing hard-copy textbooks to students via the library is one way the university can help support student success.

Additionally, there are some complexities to the hard-copy-only program. For example, many textbooks that are electronic, or multimedia textbooks that have an accompanying disc, or are hybrid (partly hard copy with online supplements) feature copyright restrictions and may not be available for library reserve. Other challenges involve considerations for older editions and parameters for new edition replacements. How long do you keep an older edition on reserve, and how many? How many new editions do you buy when the older edition is one or two years old and essentially identical? When does the edition become obsolete? Other challenges include limited checkout times, and copy availability at the students' time of need. Despite potential limitations, Kent State University Libraries (KSUL) initiated the core textbooks on reserve (CTR) program in 2012. How do we assess the value of the service? How does this service affect student success? To find out, KSUL librarians analyzed circulation data and conducted a survey to learn about the CTR program's impact on the student community and discover ways in which we might make improvements to the program.

BACKGROUND

In the fall of 2011, the KSU provost convened a Textbook Affordability Task Force charged with developing new ways to reduce the cost of textbooks for students. The task force issued the following two proposals to be enacted at the department level: (1) standardize all textbooks and course materials for Kent core courses, and (2) articulate clear textbook and course materials selection strategies for all courses with an annual enrollment of 200 or more. Although an imperative was issued for all departments to comply, the imperative was soon dropped as were the high-level conversations on the textbook cost dilemma. The primary reason the initiative did not succeed was that the faculty wished to retain autonomy in the selection of materials for their classrooms and were concerned that course material normalization would impede academic freedom.

In an effort to better support KSU students, the libraries initiated a pilot CTR program in fall 2012. The CTR program provided access to print textbooks for short-term use. A textbook must satisfy all of the following selection requirements in order to be purchased for the program:

1. The course is a basic requirement of the degree program or is an undergraduate, general course requirement referred to as Kent core curriculum
2. The course has multiple sections
3. The course has high enrollment, and the textbook is expensive

In November 2012 the libraries obtained a list of core courses and enrollment numbers for the 2013 spring semester from the registrar. The associated textbook information (title, edition, course number, price, and so on) was obtained from the campus bookstore. By cross-tabulating this data, librarians identified the titles and created a selection list for the spring 2013 pilot program. Once the program began, acquisition staff simply used the registrars' online system to identify titles that met program criteria.

The library supports the program with the collections budget. The program is in place for its third consecutive year, during which time KSUL spent a total of $36,850 on hard-copy textbooks. The 2013 spring semester pilot started in

January with a budget of $10,000 to purchase a small number of textbooks intended to gauge demand and effectiveness. In FY 2014 KSUL allocated $40,000 to ramp up support for the program but only ended up spending $18,800. In FY 2015 KSUL then allocated $20,000 and spent $11,424 and most recently in FY 2016 allocated $12,000 but only spent $7,348. The costs for textbooks ranged anywhere from $5.75 to $826.00 per book. We made some exceptions for low-cost required texts, but the average cost per textbook was $90.00.

Project orders occur twice a year, in early August and early December. In general, one copy is purchased per 100 students enrolled in a course. Records for hard-copy reserves are accessible via the reserves module in KSUL's integrated library system, KentLINK. The module can be searched by the teacher's name, the course name, or course number. Each bibliographic record contains a MARC field 793 with the phrase "Core Textbook," which makes it easy to generate a list of textbooks available.

METHODOLOGY

In spring 2016, a library survey was distributed to students enrolled in a total of 132 sections of undergraduate, general education courses, otherwise referred to as core courses with textbooks on reserve. In order to fill gaps in our knowledge of the program's effectiveness, we asked questions regarding awareness, use, satisfaction, and suggestions for improvement. Circulation data on these core textbooks was also taken into account to better understand the use of the program. We applied both qualitative and quantitative analysis methods in the study and used the SPSS Statistics program (version 22) to perform statistical data analysis. Descriptive statistic data analysis was computed on the nominal level data. We use content analysis to analyze the qualitative data from open-ended questions.

SURVEY PARTICIPANTS

The target participants of the current study were the students enrolled in the core courses that were a part of the core textbook on reserve program at Kent State University during the spring semester. The researchers obtained human subject approval from the Kent State University Institutional Review Board. We distributed an e-mail invitation with the web link for the survey to the instructors who taught these courses, asking for their assistance in distributing the survey URL to their students. The survey was administrated online in mid-April and opened for three weeks before the semester ended in mid-May 2016.

INSTRUMENT

The researchers developed the survey to assess the following: (1) students' awareness and perception of the CTR program, (2) the ways that students acquire textbooks for the core courses, and (3) the frequency of textbook usage through the CTR program. Nine questions with branched follow-up questions were included in the survey. Survey questions consisted of dichotomous questions and open-ended questions. All questions were optional and voluntary so that participants were not forced to respond to the questions they did not feel like answering. The survey was hosted online using a universal URL. No identification was collected and linked to survey data; therefore, if a participant left the survey and returned later, the system would not recognize that participant as the same respondent but instead record him or her as a separate entry.

The researchers distributed the survey to instructors who then chose their own method of distribution. They may have delivered the URL through an oral announcement in class, in a learning management system, or through class e-mail. Both survey distribution (through instructors) and participation were voluntary. We do not know if all instructors distributed the survey invitation.

We received 294 responses to the CTR survey invitation, and 238 of these were eligible as defined by answering more than one question other than the consent agreement, and were counted as valid responses. Of the respondents who agreed to participate, 56 respondents did not answer any questions, which were considered invalid survey responses. We do not know the reasons why 56 respondents to the invitation did not complete or answer any questions. It could be because they changed their mind, a technical issue, or they decided to respond later. Regardless of the possible reasons, the valid rate of the current survey is 81 percent. All analysis was based on 238 valid responses.

CIRCULATION STATISTICS

There were 81 titles and 133 copies on reserve in the CTR program in spring 2016. Circulation statistics were calculated and analyzed as part of the program (see figure 7.1). Data includes the number of times the book was checked out and what course the book supported. Because the system cannot log circulation data by date, circulation statistics for core textbooks on reserve are handled differently than routine circulating materials. Instead, circulation staff tally the data manually and the circulation data along with course number and semester information are recorded in a note field in the item record. This method of tabulating the data is tedious but accurate for the time period for each item. Based on the circulation rate per available copies, circulation totaled 1,046, with art history (22.7), marketing (17), communications (15.2), journalism (14.5), and digital science (11.2) having the highest circulation rates. Since circulation statistics are an indicator of textbook demand or popularity, these data sets could help the library target outreach efforts and plan funding.

SUBJECT	NO. OF COPIES ON RESERVE	SPRING SEMESTER CIRCULATION	NO. OF CIRCULATION PER COPY
Art History	7	159	22.71
Marketing	1	17	17.00
Communications	5	76	15.20
Journalism	4	58	14.50
Digital Sciences	10	112	11.20
History	15	129	8.60
Geography	4	34	8.50
English	15	121	8.07
Psychology	10	78	7.80
Sociology	10	74	7.40
Anthropology	1	7	7.00
Biology	7	43	6.14
Physics	6	35	5.83
Mathematics	6	28	4.67
Gerontology	1	4	4.00
Chemistry	10	36	3.60
Geology	3	8	2.67
Theatre	6	14	2.33
Philosophy	5	10	2.00
Economics	2	2	1.00
Nutrition	1	1	1.00

Figure 7.1 | **Circulation Statistics**

RESULTS

Descriptive of Respondents

The total number of students enrolled in core courses for which core textbooks were made available was around 5,500. Some students enrolled in more than one core course at a time. According to the academic program guide, most core course requirements are designed to be taken during the first two years (freshman and sophomore). As shown in figure 7.2, the number of core courses taken simultaneously each semester ranges from one to four. During the freshman and sophomore years each student is likely enrolled, on average, for about three core courses simultaneously.

We conducted the survey in spring 2015, while the CTR program supported 49 courses in 17 academic programs (as shown in figure 7.3), and a total of 238 valid respondents were from 23 courses. We received more than 20 responses from four courses each. These were general psychology (31 responses),

DEGREE PROGRAM	SEM 1	SEM 2	SEM 3	SEM 4	SEM 5	SEM 6	SEM 7	SEM 8
Anthropology	3	4	3	4	2	0	0	0
Chemistry	5	5	5	5	5	4	1	0
Communications	5	5	5	4	2	2	1	1
Digital Science	4	5	4	4	3	3	1	0
Economics	3	3	4	3	4	1	0	1
English	3	4	4	3	3	1	1	0
Geography	5	4	5	1	3	0	0	1
Geology	4	5	5	3	2	0	2	0
History	2	4	4	2	2	0	0	1
Journalism	5	5	3	2	3	1	1	1
Mathematics	3	3	3	3	5	1	0	0
Nutrition	5	5	5	5	3	5	4	4
Philosophy	3	4	4	2	2	0	0	0
Physics	3	2	3	4	5	3	4	0
Psychology	3	4	4	4	3	2	1	1
Sociology	3	4	4	4	3	3	1	0
Theatre	5	5	4	4	3	4	4	2
AVERAGE	3.76	4.18	4.06	3.35	3.12	1.76	1.24	0.71

Figure 7.2 | **Number of Core Courses in Each Bachelor's Degree Program**

ENROLLED COURSE NAME	FREQUENCY (n = 238)
General Psychology	31
Life on Planet Earth	29
Child Psychology	27
Science of Human Nutrition	21
Art as a World Phenomenon	16
Principles of Macroeconomics	14
Music as a World Phenomenon	12
Media, Power and Culture	11
Art History: Renaissance to Modern Art	9
General College Physics I	9
Introduction to Philosophy	8
Introduction to Ethics	8
College Writing II	6
How the Earth Works	6
Human Biology	5
Chemistry in Our World	5
The Art of the Theatre	5
Foundation of Chemistry	3
Criticism of Public Discourse	3
Introduction to Sociology	3
Principles of Macroeconomics	2
Introduction to Human Communication	1
Basic Mathematical Concepts II	1
Unknown	3

Figure 7.3 | **Courses Represented in the Survey**

life on planet earth (29 responses), child psychology (27 responses), and science of human nutrition (21 responses). Of the 238 respondents, about 93 percent of them were full-time students taking nine or more credit hours at the time of the survey. About 60 percent of the students indicated they have student loans (figure 7.4).

	FREQUENCY (*n* = 238)	PERCENTAGE (%)
Enrolled Credit Hours		
1–8 (Part–time)	3	1.3
9–19 (Full–time)	221	92.8
Did not answer	14	5.9
Student Loan		
Have one	140	58.8
Without one	83	34.9
Did not answer	15	6.3

Figure 7.4 | **Respondent Characteristics**

WAYS TO ACQUIRE TEXTBOOKS

Renting (62) and purchasing (62) a new copy of a textbook were the two most common methods that students used to acquire textbooks for a course, while using library copies (12) was the least common way to acquire textbooks (figure 7.5). For those who bought or rented textbooks, the results show that online retailers (75) and the Kent State Student Center Bookstore (66) were the two main resources that students used to purchase or rent the textbooks for their courses, followed by an off-campus bookstore (10), and then friends (6). Online retailers such as Amazon and Chegg were the top two websites/retailers that students use to acquire textbooks (figure 7.6).

When questioned about the amount of money that participants spent on textbooks for the current course, about 27 percent indicated that they spent nothing and 20 percent indicated

METHODS	FREQUENCY
Purchase	62
Rent	62
Did not Acquire Textbook(s)	43
Other	27
Borrow from Friends	17
Use Library Copies	12

Figure 7.5 | **Methods for Acquiring Textbooks**

RESOURCES	FREQUENCY
Online Retailer	75
Kent State Student Center Bookstore	66
Off Campus Store	10
Friend or Other Students	6

Figure 7.6 | **Resources of Textbook Acquisition**

they spent between $26 and $50. Nearly half of the participants stated that for all courses in the semester their expenditure was between $100 and $300. Those surveyed also indicated that $50 per course was a reasonable cost for textbooks.

AWARENESS AND THE USE OF THE CTR PROGRAM

More than half (57.6 percent) of the respondents indicated that, before they took the survey, they did not know some textbooks could be checked out from the library (figure 7.7). For those aware of the program, approximately 60 percent of respondents pointed out that the instructor was the primary resource by which students learned that textbooks for some courses could be checked out through the CTR program, followed by classmates (20.8 percent) and then librarians (14.8 percent) (figure 7.8).

When asking students about their textbook checkout experience, only 5 percent of respondents indicated that they checked out a textbook through the CTR program. The results further showed that students usually checked out a textbook 2–5 times during the semester. Open-ended questions following the initial questions revealed that some of the reasons for less-frequent use were that they only needed it once, the two-hour loan period was too short, and that CTR textbooks' availability and location were inconvenient (i.e., can't leave library with the book; only available when the circulation desk is open).

The survey also asked the general students' opinion regarding the CTR program. Based on the students' comments, the overall attitude towards

	FREQUENCY (n = 238)	PERCENTAGE (%)
Know the Program	101	42.4
Did not Know the Program	137	57.6

Figure 7.7 | **Awareness of the CTR Program**

	FREQUENCY (n = 101)	PERCENTAGE (%)
Sources		
Instructor	62	61.4
Classmates/Friends	21	20.8
Libraries/Librarians	15	14.8
Other	3	3.0

Figure 7.8 | **Source of Learning about the CTR Program**

the CTR program was positive. They welcome the CTR program in supporting students' textbook demands. Limited book quantity and limited time length for checkout were the two common themes found in the negative responses.

TEXTBOOK COST ON ENROLLMENT DECISION

The survey further asked if the cost of textbooks affected students' choice for course registration. As shown in figure 7.9, we found that about 57 percent of students indicated the cost of textbooks will not influence their decision for course enrollment, while nearly 37 percent of respondents indicated that the cost of textbooks does in fact influence their course enrollment decision.

Q: WOULD YOU EVER BE DISCOURAGED TO REGISTER FOR A COURSE WITH EXPENSIVE BOOKS?	FREQUENCY (n = 238)	PERCENTAGE (%)
Yes	88	37.0
No	136	57.1
Did not answer	14	5.9

Figure 7.9 | **Impact on Course Enrollment Decision**

We asked participants: "In what way does the cost of textbooks influence your decision to enroll (or not enroll) in a course?" The survey elicited 71 responses, with many expressing frustration with the financial burden. For example: "I will usually enroll, but often will not buy the textbook." or "If I can't afford the textbook, I can't be successful in the class and learn the material I was meant to learn."

In general, the responses to the follow-up questions regarding how textbook costs affect enrollment decisions are interesting. Overall, two major themes emerged from students' responses: (1) the cost did not matter because they did not buy/acquire textbook for classes, and (2) courses are required for the program completion. In other words, the cost of textbooks does matter. Students appear to have come up with these two approaches in handling their textbook issues: either take up the burden no matter what the cost because it's required to complete the program, or else do not buy the books.

CONCLUSION

So what have we learned from this exercise, what issues have been identified, and what are possible ways in which we might make improvements to the program?

The results indicate successful use for some courses, but we know that more than half of the students surveyed were not aware of the CTR program. We may conclude from this that more promotion is needed in order to make the best use of the program. While continuing to communicate the CTR program to students through instructors and librarians, we need to think of other effective ways to get the word out. One possible method is to display or link the CRT textbook information to the registration (course sign-up) which would catch students' attention at the point of need. Consistent reminders of the CTR through library instruction sections, information tables at university-hosted events, and fliers all contribute to awareness.

The data shows that of those aware of the service, only 5 percent actually used the CTR program. Although the number of students who use the program appears low, library circulation figures are more encouraging and indicate the service is useful for some students. Of the 133 textbook copies on reserve, only 3 percent had no circulation at all, 50 percent had more than two checkouts, and 100 percent of the unique titles circulated at least once. Compare this with the average circulation of the general KSUL collection, where 40 percent never circulates. From this point of view, the CTR collection is a good return on investment for the library.

Additionally, we can extrapolate the hypothetical savings for students by examining the circulation during the 2016 spring semester. In one semester, 1,046 checkouts could mean that KSUL potentially helped 1,046 students, saving them on average $90 each, for a total student savings of $94,140. Presume the same for the 2016 fall semester, and it's logical to infer that KSUL saved students about $188,000 in textbook expenses in the 2016 academic year. Even if the reality is half that, the amount of savings is still significant.

One of the more interesting survey outcomes describes how many students acquire textbooks. The data shows that although most students acquire textbooks through purchase or rental, some borrow or find the textbooks for "free" online. Thirty-seven percent expressed hesitance to register for a course if it required expensive textbooks, and a significant number stated that they do not buy textbooks at all. Although we cannot tell exactly why some students did not spend any money on textbooks, we can speculate that students may (1) be using pirated materials, (2) use an older edition library copy, (3) use a copy belonging to a friend, or (4) simply do not use a textbook at all. Any of these circumstances is less than ideal and should raise a red flag among university administration, faculty, and librarians alike. It is also disconcerting that students might resort to illegal means of acquiring needed textbooks by using pirated materials. According to the literature, few students obtain all learning materials legally, with the most common reason being high costs.[8]

The data reveals that students are not obtaining the textbooks required for their success in their courses because of the cost. While students find creative ways to obtain textbooks such as borrowing a friend's book, opting not to use the book, using a library copy, or possibly pirating books, all of these scenarios have an impact on student learning due to limited access to necessary learning materials. Since we know that there is a direct correlation between student success and the ability to access the required course materials, this information raises serious concerns about how we support our students.

Looking forward, it might be worthwhile to expand the scope of the program to provide service for a larger user base. Purchasing additional copies of high-demand textbooks may allow for longer checkout periods. Although cost is a factor here, historical spending patterns show that the program costs are less than anticipated and have stabilized over time. Other questions about the CTR service itself suggest possible barriers to use. The short two-hour loan period, the inconvenient time and location, the inability to leave the library with the book, and the fact that access is limited to those hours when the library is open are a few of the reasons cited for less-frequent use. Some possible solutions to the availability issue include longer checkout times; an advance reservation service that allows students to better arrange their study schedules; and making additional copies available. Despite its limitations, we believe that the CTR program has merit. Not only is the program validated by circulation statistics and students' positive comments, but it offers an alternative choice of textbook access for KSU students.

Notes

1. Amy Chang and Judy Garrison, "Textbook Lending Service," *College & Research Libraries News* 72, no. 4 (2011): 527–30; Julie Middlemas, Patricia Morrison, and Nadra Farina-Hess, "Reserve Textbooks," *Library Philosophy and Practice* (September 2012): 1–9.

2. James A. Buczynski, "Faculty Begin to Replace Textbooks with 'Freely' Accessible Online Resources," *Internet Reference Services Quarterly* 11, no. 4 (2007): 169–79;

Michael B. Paulsen and Edward P. St. John, "Social Class and College Costs: Examining the Financial Nexus between College Choice and Persistence," *Journal of Higher Education* 73, no. 2 (2002): 189–236.

3. Buczynski, "Faculty."

4. Charles Lyons, "Library Roles with Textbook Affordability," *Against the Grain* 26, no. 5 (2014): 1–6.

5. D. Gibbs and J. Bowdoin, "TextSelect: Purchasing Textbooks for Library Reserves," *Against the Grain* 26, no. 5 (2014): 34–36.

6. Osman Celik and Roxanne Peck, "If You Expand, They Will Come: Textbook Affordability through Expansion of Course Reserves: The Case of UCLA Library's Course Reserves via Strategic Partnership with the Campus Independent Bookstore," *Technical Services Quarterly* 33, no. 3 (2016): 268–78.

7. Donald A. Barclay, "No Reservations: Why the Time Has Come to Kill Print Textbook Reserves," *College & Research Libraries News* 76 (2015): 332–35.

8. Laura Czerniewicz, "Student Practices in Copyright Culture: Accessing Learning Resources," *Learning Media and Technology* (2016): 7, 11–15, doi: 10.1080/17439884 .2016.1160928; Tim Cushing, "Study Indicates College Textbook Piracy Is on the Rise, but Fails to Call Out Publishers for Skyrocketing Prices," Techdirt (2014), https:// www.techdirt.com/articles/20140921/19385328596/study-indicates-college-textbook -piracy-is-rise-fails-to-call-out-publishers-skyrocketing-prices.shtml; M. L. Nestel and Ryan Walsh, "Why College Students Are Stealing Their Textbooks," Vocativ (2014), www.vocativ.com/usa/education-usa/lots-college-students-simply-stopped-paying -textbooks/.

Bibliography

Barclay, Donald A. "No Reservations: Why the Time Has Come to Kill Print Textbook Reserves." *College & Research Libraries News* 76 (June 2015): 332–35. http://crln.acrl .org/content/76/6/332.full.

Buczynski, James A. "Faculty Begin to Replace Textbooks with 'Freely' Accessible Online Resources." *Internet Reference Services Quarterly* 11, no. 4 (2007): 169–79. http://dx.doi .org/10.1300/J136v11n04_11.

Celik, Osman, and Roxanne Peck. "If You Expand, They Will Come: Textbook Affordability through Expansion of Course Reserves: The Case of UCLA Library's Course Reserves via Strategic Partnership with the Campus Independent Bookstore." *Technical Services Quarterly* 33, no. 3 (2016): 268–78. http://dx.doi.org/10.1080/07317131.2016.1169788.

Chang, Amy, and Judy Garrison. "Textbook Lending Service: Providing a Service Students Need When They Need It." *College & Research Libraries News* 72, no. 9 (2011): 527–30. http://crln.acrl.org/content/72/9/527.full.

Cushing, Tim. "Study Indicates College Textbook Piracy Is on the Rise, but Fails to Call Out Publishers for Skyrocketing Prices." Techdirt. 2014. https://www.techdirt.com/articles/20140921/19385328596/study-indicates-college-textbook-piracy-is-rise-fails-to-call-out-publishers-skyrocketing-prices.shtml.

Czerniewicz, Laura. "Student Practices in Copyright Culture: Accessing Learning Resources." *Learning Media and Technology*. 2016. doi: 10.1080/17439884.2016.1160928.

Gibbs, D., and J. Bowdoin. "TextSelect: Purchasing Textbooks for Library Reserves." *Against the Grain* 26, no. 5 (2014): 34–36.

Lyons, Charles. "Library Roles with Textbook Affordability." *Against the Grain* 26, no. 5 (2014): 1–6.

Middlemas, Julie, Patricia Morrison, and Nadra Farina-Hess. "Reserve Textbooks: To Buy, or Not to Buy?" *Library Philosophy and Practice* (September 2012): 1–9. http://digitalcommons.unl.edu/libphilprac/796/.

Nestel, M. L., and Ryan Walsh. "Why College Students Are Stealing Their Textbooks." Vocativ. 2014. www.vocativ.com/usa/education-usa/lots-college-students-simply-stopped-paying-textbooks/.

Paulsen, Michael B., and Edward P. St. John. "Social Class and College Costs: Examining the Financial Nexus between College Choice and Persistence." *Journal of Higher Education* 73, no. 2 (2002): 189–236. www.jstor.org/stable/1558410.

8

WALKING THE TIGHTROPE
Balancing Students' Desire for Textbooks and the Library Budget

Rhonda Glazier and Carla Myers

The circulation of college textbooks through academic library reserve services has long been a contentious issue. Some libraries have readily embraced the practice, some strictly forbid it, and the remaining institutions usually circulate textbooks on a case-by-case basis. While the circulation of textbooks is often heartily embraced by students, it does pose certain problems for academic libraries, including:

- Which textbooks will be acquired?
- If the library will be purchasing the books, what funds are available to support this practice?
- Will multiple copies of the most popular textbooks be acquired?
- How will circulation parameters such as length of checkout time be determined?

This chapter will explore how one academic library launched a reserve textbook checkout service and their answers to these questions.

ABOUT THE KRAEMER FAMILY LIBRARY

The Kraemer Family Library (KFL) serves the University of Colorado Colorado Springs (UCCS) campus community, which includes approximately 11,000 on-campus students and another 2,000 students enrolled in online courses (University of Colorado Colorado Springs, 2015).[1] For the 2014–15 fiscal year the library had a materials expenditure budget of $1,866,136. The library currently has over 407,000 print volumes in its collection and has approximately 32 employees, 5 of whom work in Circulation, 1.5 staff members in Acquisitions, and 3 in the Cataloging Department. There are currently 11 librarians on staff who have collection development responsibilities. In FY 2015 the library had more than 860,000 patron visits and 90,400 item circulations.[2]

THE KRAEMER FAMILY LIBRARY AND TEXTBOOK ACQUISITIONS

For many years KFL shied away from offering textbooks through its reserve service. While there was no formal collection development policy in place that prohibited the acquisition of textbooks for the collection, librarians were actively encouraged to not purchase textbooks so that the library would not set unrealistic expectations for students. The major concern voiced during this time was that the library would not be able to purchase all the titles being used in classes across campus, and therefore the library should not set up unrealistic expectations by offering "some." The result was that most librarians did not purchase textbooks unless specifically asked to do so by a course instructor.

Even though librarians were encouraged to not purchase textbooks, the library did own and circulate a few random titles. Some instructors lent the library their own personal copies of textbooks that were placed on reserve and circulated to students. Other textbooks on reserve were titles acquired "by accident." In other words, if a title that met the scope of the collection was purchased and it happened to be a title that a professor required for a class, it could be placed on reserve. Unfortunately, this set up a situation where the library was inadvertently supporting some classes by having the textbook available while ignoring other classes. Primarily, it created situations where students in the humanities would have access to some of their course materials—plays, poetry collections, and other literature that was purchased by the library—while students in the hard sciences or business area were less likely to find materials required for their courses in the library. Adding to this problem was the fact that there was no effort to systematically identify items in the library's collection that were being used for course instruction and proactively place them on reserve. This resulted in some savvy students checking out these items from the library well before the semester started. When the course instructor later learned that the library owned the course materials and requested that they be recalled and placed on reserve, the circulation staff often had trouble getting the student to return the items. Sometimes these items were checked out through interlibrary loan or the Colorado library consortium, Prospector, and then it would be even more difficult for the library to recall the items in a timely manner in order to make them available for UCCS students. As a result, accessing what few textbooks the library did own was often a frustrating experience for both students and course instructors.

This informal policy of not purchasing textbooks was in place until 2010. At that time a librarian who had experience circulating textbooks through reserve became the head of the Access Services Department and began to examine ways to expand this service. At first, this involved tracking student requests for textbook titles and then approaching the instructor for these courses to see if he or she owned a copy of the book that could be placed on reserve. It also involved the intentional purchase of the required textbooks for several lower-division, high-enrollment courses in business and economics, this librarian's collection development areas. With the initial success of the program, several other librarians began purchasing textbooks for lower-division, high-enrollment courses in their subject areas as well.

At the end of the first semester of this informal project, the circulation statistics for all of the textbooks that were on reserve in each subject area were shared with the librarians who had purchased textbooks for their subject area. The circulation statistics for the personal copies of textbooks that were on loan to the library by instructors were included alongside those that had been purchased as part of this project. Based on the circulation statistics, almost all of the librarians who were participating in this project decided to purchase textbooks for additional lower-division, high-enrollment courses, and some even began purchasing textbooks for higher-division courses. Statistics for all of these titles were tracked and evaluated by the subject librarians and circulation staff each semester. This initial pilot project was formalized in 2015 with six of the eleven librarians purchasing textbooks for reserve. While there have been adjustments made over the years, most of the librarians who are participating in the textbook program are happy with the results.

LESSONS LEARNED

Textbook Identification and Use Tracking

In this project's infancy, the only way to determine what titles instructors were using was to obtain a copy of the course syllabus or use the UCCS Bookstore's website to identify what titles were being sold for each course. Frustrated with trying to identify textbook titles piecemeal, the head of Access Services contacted the campus bookstore and asked if they would be willing to provide the library with a list of the course textbooks for the entire campus each semester. They readily agreed. The list is provided to the Circulation Department about forty-five days before the start of each semester. The circulation staff divide the list by subject area and search each title in the library's catalog first by ISBN and then, if no results are found, by title. A note is added to the list if the library owns the item, if it is the current edition being used or a previous edition, the location of the item (currently on reserve, reference, circulating collection, etc.), and the status of the item (available, checked out, missing, billed, etc.). If the item is not owned, the circulation staff looks the item up on Amazon .com and notes the selling price. This information is passed along to the subject librarians who are interested in purchasing textbooks in their subject areas, and allows them to make an informed choice on whether or not to keep the item on reserve, place it on reserve, or to acquire a copy of the work to add to the reserve collection. This proactive approach of identifying, acquiring, and placing textbooks on reserve was beneficial to students, primarily because many of the questions and requests for textbook titles occur right before the semester starts, or during the first two weeks. By having these materials in the catalog before the peak demand time, we were able to accurately inform a student looking for a textbook about whether or not we have that title.

Some UCCS instructors continue to provide personal copies of textbooks to circulate on reserve, and these are readily accepted. As each semester gets underway, the circulation staff monitors the circulation counts of textbooks. When books are being checked out more than five times a week for several weeks straight, the subject librarian is notified that the item is in high demand. One of the greatest indicators that multiple copies of a textbook are needed is when numerous students ask for the title in the course of a day, but are unable to access it because it is constantly checked out. Subject librarians are also notified when this occurs so that they can consider purchasing a second, or even a third copy of the title to meet this high level of demand. When students inquire about a title that the library does not currently own, the information for the item and course are documented and the information is made available to the subject librarians. There have been times when a librarian initially chose not to purchase a particular textbook but, due to popular demand, changed her mind.

Purchasing

Once the library decided to purchase select textbooks, a process needed to be put in place to make sure that copies were received and cataloged before the beginning of each semester. Acquisitions needed to know at the time of order that the book being ordered is a textbook and will be going on reserve. Since these are titles that will be used in the classroom during the semester, the chance that a hold would be placed on the title before receipt is very likely. To get around this problem, a "patron" was set up in the system for reserve and at the time of order, a hold is placed using this account. By placing the hold at the time of ordering, the library is guaranteed to be the first "patron" to get the book. If other patrons have placed a hold before the book is received, these holds are canceled and the patrons are notified that the item is on reserve.

In many cases the library does not have the list of textbooks being used until a few weeks before the semester. To keep these materials moving, all textbook orders are marked RUSH so that they are ordered first, and the vendor to purchase the title from is chosen based on availability, not price. Once the title is received it will then be rushed through cataloging and processing and taken down to circulation within forty-eight hours of receipt. The primary advantage to rushing these materials through technical services is that the title shows up in the catalog almost immediately, and is placed on reserve quickly, so that students looking for a textbook know it is available, and for how long.

Collection Development

As the library began purchasing textbooks on a more proactive basis, it became clear that the library needed to decide whether or not a formal collection development policy on textbooks needed to be established. As expected, there were good reasons for creating a collection development policy, and there were also arguments presented on why not having a formal policy may work best. Some of the collection development issues that kept coming up over and over had to do with the very nature of textbooks. In many cases, extra content such as study guides and quizzes is included electronically and the textbook would have an activation code needed to access that information. Many of the librarians selecting textbooks were informally deciding not to purchase titles with extra content that would be limited to one user. But others did not make a distinction and would purchase a title with online content that had limited use. There were also cases where acquisitions staff were unclear about whether or not a specific title included this extra content. It was determined that preference would be given to editions that do not include extra online content unless that content could be used by multiple users. When a librarian selects a title with online content, acquisitions staff at the time of receipt will remove the information on how to access the online content if it is limited to one user. If the online content is available through a code that can be used by more than one person, the information is left with the book.

Another area of concern was the cost of these titles. Many of the textbooks being selected cost $200 or $300. Some librarians had budgets with enough money to absorb the purchase of textbooks, while other librarians were concerned that one or two textbooks could wipe out their entire book budget. Because the library does not have a collection development policy limiting the amount of money that can be spent on any given title, collection development librarians can spend any amount that they feel necessary for any title, and are responsible for balancing the cost of purchasing the textbook with other titles available in that subject area.

After working through these issues around textbooks, KFL decided against a formal collection development policy on textbooks. This was primarily because many of the issues could be handled with a procedure, for example, removing information on online access content, and a comprehensive definition of textbook would be almost impossible to determine. In the end, the library decided that limiting what titles an individual librarian could purchase for her subject area was counterproductive.

Budget

Budget constraints are focusing how funds are being spent, and each librarian has the flexibility to purchase textbooks for her area if that is the greatest need in her subject area. KFL has experienced flat to minimal growth in the materials budget over the last three years. In FY 2014 a little under 26 percent of the materials budget was spent on print materials. By FY 2016 that percentage was down to a little over 20 percent. This means that each subject librarian has received a smaller allocation for print materials each fiscal year. This decrease is offset by the number of patron-driven acquisition e-book programs managed by the library. The library is actively adding discovery records to the library's catalog, and most subject librarians are not purchasing in print titles that are available electronically. Interestingly, with the e-book programs many subject librarians are finding it difficult to spend their print funds, and having the option to purchase textbooks that they know will be used has helped. Over the years this has resulted in the liaisons for areas such as business, math, and science spending more of their funds on textbooks and the liaisons for subject areas in the arts and English spending less.

When comparing the average cost of books purchased for each subject area over the past three years, the increase in the cost of books has been anywhere from no increase to a 23 percent increase over that three-year period. Cost increases were higher for the subject areas where textbooks were purchased. However, there were subject areas where textbooks were purchased that had little or no increase; for example, chemistry. Moreover, some subject areas had higher-than-average increases even though only a few textbooks were purchased; for example, art. Figure 8.1 gives representative increases across subject areas and whether or not textbooks were purchased in that subject area.

PURCHASING TEXTBOOKS	AVERAGE YEARLY INCREASE (%)
BUSINESS	23
BIOLOGY	5
CHEMISTRY	—

PURCHASING LIMITED NUMBER OF TEXTBOOKS	AVERAGE YEARLY INCREASE (%)
MUSIC	11
THEATER	6
ART	11
MECHANICAL ENGINEERING	4

NOT PURCHASING TEXTBOOKS	AVERAGE YEARLY INCREASE (%)
NURSING	—
COMPUTER SCIENCE	3
POLITICAL SCIENCE	8
ANTHROPOLOGY	1

Figure 8.1 | **Representative Subject Areas, Percentage Increase by Textbook Purchasing Decision, FY2014–FY2016**

To put these numbers in context, the average increase across all disciplines was 2 percent each year.

It should be noted that subject librarians have not indicated a lack of funds. Most librarians are adding materials throughout the year and are not running out of money before the end of the fiscal year. That being said, as more of the librarians choose to purchase textbooks, the rate of cost increase will need to be managed. The library is hoping to use resource sharing such as interlibrary loan or the statewide shared catalog Prospector for titles that would be considered secondary to the curriculum and research needs of the university. It is clear that reserve books are being used, and finding ways to move secondary titles to "just in time" will allow the library to manage the cost increases. We are also looking at gift funds and auxiliary accounts to supplement the cost of textbooks. In general, the budget question becomes what level of secondary materials does the library want to maintain, instead of not purchasing textbooks that we know will be used by students.

MANAGING EXPECTATIONS

As the library's reserve service grew in popularity, the staff found that many members of the campus community had mistaken expectations of the service that included item availability, placing items on reserve, and circulation periods.

Item Availability

Many students and instructors mistakenly believe that the library acquires every textbook in use on campus. Some instructors who were under this impression would tell students on the first day of class that the library had their textbook available when in fact it was not. When these students would ask for their book, they often became frustrated and angry to learn it was not available. To combat this problem, a LibGuide was developed to help students better understand the library's reserve textbooks circulation service. It outlines the circulation periods of reserve items, highlights the fact that we do not own every textbook, and guides students through the process of searching for their particular course texts.

Placing Items on Reserve

Some instructors proactively check the library's catalog to see if we already own course materials, but after discovering that we do own the item they failed to place a request for it to be placed on reserve. Inevitably the item gets checked out under normal loan rules by a UCCS student who is enrolled in their class, or is requested by a patron from a library in the statewide consortium or through interlibrary loan. Other times an instructor will ask a subject librarian to purchase a film or book he intends to use as part of course instruction, but he does not convey this intent to the librarian. Consequently, the item does not get placed on reserve and it may not be available when they need it. To encourage instructors to be proactive in placing items on reserve, information on the reserve submission process was placed on the library's website. Periodic e-mail reminders about how to place items on reserve are also sent out over a campus discussion list.

Circulation Periods

When students first check out a reserve item, many are surprised to find that it only circulates for two or four hours and not the normal three-to-six-week circulation period they are accustomed to. While information regarding these circulation periods is included in our LibGuide, most of our education on this misconception occurs in person. Most students come to understand this practice once the circulation staff explains that the shorter circulation periods are used for reserve items in order to allow as many students as possible to access the item.

PROGRAM EXPANSION

We have seen an increase in the number of students in junior and senior-level classes inquiring whether or not the library has a copy of their textbook. The circulation staff was initially surprised by the increased number of requests for these higher-level textbooks, but then realized that the students asking for these books were those who had started as freshmen at UCCS as the library's textbook acquisition program was gaining steam. Having become accustomed to the library having many of their lower-level textbooks available, they were surprised to learn that many of the higher-level textbooks were not actively being purchased as well. As a result, more attention has been given to text-books for the higher-level courses, and some librarians have begun purchasing textbooks for required higher-level courses where there is a lot of demand for the textbook.

In addition to asking for textbooks, many students began to ask if other resources they needed for their courses were available for checkout, such as graphing calculators and materials that can be used for class presentations or study, such as HDMI cables, clickers, dry erase boards (8.5 × 11 in.), highlighters, headphones, and even charging cables for electronic devices. Consequently, the library began acquiring these items as well. Students' response to the program expansion has been overwhelming.

GOING FORWARD

The checkout statistics for reserve items illustrate the success of the program. For the 2013–14 academic year (August through July) there were a total of 9,269 reserve checkouts, which accounted for about 14.9 percent of the total checkouts for the library during this time. In the 2014–15 academic year the number of reserve checkouts jumped to 12,949, which accounted for about 22.3 percent of the total checkouts for the library. In the 2015–16 academic year the 19,357 reserve checkouts accounted for 30.9 percent of the total checkouts for the library during this time.

Given the positive response to this program from the campus community, those librarians who have been participating in it have been pursuing options to expand the program going forward. Ideas include:

Explore options to create a dedicated fund that can be used to acquire course materials in order to better track the cost of this program for the library. This could include textbooks as well as other items that enhance classroom learning and support the curriculum. Examples include acquiring anatomical models such as a skeleton that can be used by students studying anatomy and physiology, and acquiring molecular model kits that can be used by students studying chemistry.

Partner with the campus bookstore to acquire textbooks directly from them. In the past custom textbooks have been acquired through the campus bookstore, but most other textbooks are acquired from other vendors. Acquiring textbooks directly from the campus bookstore would cut the time needed for these items to ship from the online vendor, allowing the library to make these items available to students more quickly.

Analyze the regular circulating collection against the textbook reserve program. It is clear that reserve items, in general, have a higher circulation. It will be important to put those numbers in perspective so that the librarians who are not purchasing textbooks will be able to understand the impact that these titles have on supporting students. It is also important to analyze the impact of this program on the collection as a whole.

Build in more assessment tools. While circulation is one indicator of success, the library would like to identify assessment tools that will supplement the circulation data.

The textbook reserve has been a very popular program for KFL. It will be important to begin to systematically assess the impact of this service on the faculty, students, and library. Though still an informal endeavor, the library's textbook circulation program has generally been a success and has helped many students gain access to materials that they might not have otherwise been able to afford. At this time there are no plans to formalize the program, but there are also no plans to eliminate it. For the librarians who are acquiring textbooks and other class materials, the primary goal is to continue to do so in a way that balances the library's budget with student need.

Notes

1. University of Colorado Colorado Springs, "Facts and Figures," last modified October 2015, www.uccs.edu/about/facts.html.

2. Kraemer Family Library, "Library Statistics," www.uccs.edu/library/info/statistics.html.

Bibliography

Kraemer Family Library. "Library Statistics." www.uccs.edu/library/info/statistics.html.

University of Colorado Colorado Springs. "Facts and Figures." Last modified October 2015. www.uccs.edu/about/facts.html.

GENERAL EDUCATION

Ten Years of Textbooks at the Ohio State University Libraries

Aaron Olivera

I t is often accepted as a truism that the needs of today's undergraduate students are strikingly different from those of their predecessors. The veracity of this statement is often buttressed by some simple but real observations: the prevalence of mobile devices not only on campus but also within the classroom itself; the increased familiarity with and demand for web-based educational tools and collaborative spaces both on and offline; and a general perception of college as an economic transaction rather than a transformative intellectual experience. While the first two phenomena can certainly be traced back to the rise of the world's first "born digital" generation, the third one has actually been a prevalent mode of thought for college students since well before the twenty-first century. As a greater percentage of undergraduates began accepting a larger debt load in exchange for their degree, college affordability moved to the forefront of higher education discourse.

For undergraduate students, however, making college affordable is not solely about lobbying for tuition freezes or reining in the cost of campus meal plans; it is also about those unavoidable financial transactions that impact the savings or checking accounts of each student directly, and for many years the transaction that has become the symbol of student frustration is the cost of their required textbooks. This frustration is acute in part because it is twofold: the price of the average undergraduate textbook has been rising above inflation for many years, and the market for college textbooks suffers from the moral hazard of a principal-agent problem.[1] In this context the hazard occurs because despite the appearance of a regular supply-and-demand market, the student buying the textbook (the principal) is bound to the adoption selection made by the instructor (the agent). This, in turn, limits incentives that would normally drive prices downward and leaves students feeling powerless as they are forced to hand over a sizeable proportion of their cash-in-hand for materials whose usefulness is seen as confined to the number of weeks in a term. It was this disempowerment and the corresponding anxiety over the rising cost of an undergraduate education at the Ohio State University (OSU) that led to the creation of the General Education Curriculum (GEC) Textbook Project a decade ago.

In late 2005 representatives of the Policy Group of the university's Undergraduate Student Government (USG) took an interest in solving what they referred to as the "textbook problem." Understanding the role of the library as one that provides access to textual information, USG reached out to the OSU Libraries (OSUL) for collaboration on a project that would allow for certain textbooks adopted in large-enrollment GEC courses to be available in a campus library. Heretofore, the libraries had provided course materials via closed reserves on an ad hoc basis; individual subject librarians were free to collect these resources as they deemed appropriate, and donations were accepted from faculty who requested that their personal copy be made available to students. The USG found this arrangement lacking for multiple reasons: reserve holdings did not reflect the overall needs of the undergraduate population; closed reserve checkout was viewed as a barrier to access for patrons without knowledge of their precise course number or professor's name; variations in department library operating hours made using materials difficult for certain nontraditional students; and no outward promotion of these materials meant a dearth of awareness across campus. To assuage the latter concerns, the libraries agreed to situate this project on newly designated open reserve shelving prominently located near the entrance of the university's 24-hour Science and Engineering Library (SEL); the Textbook Project officially commenced on January 11, 2006.[2]

PHASE ONE
THE GEC TEXTBOOK PROJECT AT SEL

From a decade's distance, the premier iteration of the GEC Textbook Project appears somewhat alien to what it looks like in its current form. As mentioned above, rather than house the collection at the university's main Thompson Library, the textbooks were installed at the nearby SEL; this not only served the stated needs established by the USG, which preferred around-the-clock access to the materials, but also reflected the realities of an upcoming renovation to the flagship library building that would see its collections moved off campus for three years. Likewise, while honoring the spirit of USG's request to make the textbooks available via open reserves, certain duplicate titles and supplemental materials, like perforated workbooks and media discs, were held on closed reserves at SEL and subject to two-hour circulation intervals in order to ensure their viability.

Original funding for the project came via a one-time allotment of $20,000 from the trademark funds that the libraries receives each year per a long-standing agreement with the university to distribute income made from its successful licensing and branding regime. It was decided that going forward the annual budget for the project would be $15,000 per fiscal year, but rather than cull the necessary funds from the trademark allotment, the annual budget would come from a regular monograph acquisition fund created specifically for the project.

Selecting materials for inclusion required a small amount of compromise and a larger amount of research. Although both parties agreed that all textbooks in the collection should be adopted for courses that fulfilled a GEC requirement as established by the College of Arts and Sciences, USG's conceptual framework prioritized enrollment numbers over the retail price of the required textbook, while OSUL wanted to look at both data points equally, believing that undergraduate students would be less likely to seek out a library copy of a standard trade paperback like *Crime and Punishment* which can be purchased at the bookstore for a reasonable price. A price floor of $75 was agreed upon, meaning that only textbooks retailing for that price or greater would be considered for inclusion.

Luckily, both parties felt that an enrollment threshold of 200 students, in all combined sections of a course where appropriate, was adequate; this number is consistent with what are considered large-enrollment courses. For the first 200 students in a course, two copies of the required textbook would be acquired, with an additional copy purchased for each additional 100 students unless the library already held a copy on reserve. If the same title was assigned for a different GEC course or over a sequence of aligned courses (like Astronomy 161 and 162, which had to be taken as a multi-quarter sequence for proper GEC credit), then those enrollment figures were factored in as well. At project kickoff there were 96 textbooks on open reserve covering 48 courses.

At the libraries' discretion, each acquired item was fully cataloged and labeled, including bold stamping of the university's name on the head, tail, and fore-edge, and official "GEC Textbook" spine decals were affixed that fit with the aesthetic branding developed for the project by the libraries' graphic artist. Before hitting the shelves at SEL, each item was also fitted with a paper band around the front cover that asked users to draw a check mark upon it to indicate use prior to returning the item. Order of placement on the shelf was alphanumeric by department and then course, ranging from Anthropology 200 to Statistics 145. In an attempt at some form of narrative assessment, 8½ × 3½-inch paper surveys and a corresponding return box were placed alongside the collection to elicit voluntary responses.

Even as the GEC Textbook Project rolled out on time and to the satisfaction of both the libraries and the USG, operational challenges were already being discovered. The first issue that was encountered involved identifying exactly which textbooks were being assigned for the courses covered. OSU does not have a homegrown bookstore, relying instead on several privately owned bookstores near campus to accommodate student needs; as such there exists no "master list" of required textbooks that the libraries could use to determine which items to acquire. Additionally, the decentralization of academic departments across campus allows for each to handle its syllabi as it sees fit, which leads to an uneven distribution of textbook adoption information. For the foundational collection, USG aided the libraries with textbook identification, contacting departments and faculty directly, but this assistance was only offered at the outset and so it was left to the project's executor and staff to identify new adoptions before each subsequent quarter began.

The decision to use an open reserve shelving system for the project created additional challenges. Assessing the usefulness of the collection was difficult; the paper bands asking for check marks were mostly ignored when they were not being removed or otherwise used in a manner inconsistent with their purpose: one user took to writing homework answers on the band, while others tore pieces off to use as bookmarks. For this reason, attempts to systematically record item usage were abandoned. The voluntary surveys also quickly became more heat than light. While those who filled them out were nearly universal in their praise of the project, most greatly underestimated the financial resources of the libraries and suggested that the project expand to cover all required materials for all courses offered at the university. Combined, this left the project with little more than anecdotes and inferences from which to evaluate its success.

Without a doubt, however, the most important issue to arise during the first phase of the GEC Textbook Project was asset management. Despite security tape within and an overabundance of branding on the outside of each item, losses were heavy. Efforts to expand the number of courses covered were stymied as a greater percentage of the annual budget went to replacement copies of items purchased previously; in 2008 alone the project lost over $8,000 worth of materials. Although there was never a definitive answer to the question of why such high losses were occurring, the Occam's razor would suppose that open reserve availability, proximity of the collection to SEL's entrance, and the known cash value of used textbooks all combined to make theft an appealing possibility for those willing to risk the consequences. On two occasions the libraries were notified by a local bookstore that an item with the libraries' branding had been offered up for buyback, but neither instance led to a return of the material in question. The problem became so acute that the university's student newspaper published an article imploring readers to cease removing textbooks lest the project be terminated.[3]

As resource expansion choked on the budget realities that came with an unsecured and valuable print collection and a dearth of quantitative data left the project without a voice to argue for its perpetual existence, by 2009 it became clear to the libraries that in order for the GEC Textbook Project to survive it would need to adapt.

PHASE TWO
THE GEC TEXTBOOK PROJECT MOVES TO THE THOMPSON LIBRARY

Luckily for the GEC Textbook Project, 2009 was a major transitional year for the libraries at Ohio State. As mentioned above, the flagship Thompson Library, under renovation since 2006, was reopened with the Business, Journalism and Sullivant library collections merged into it as those spaces were repurposed. With the GEC Textbook Project stalling under its original mandates, the libraries considered a restart that would not only allow for a more secure collection and better analysis, but would also have synergy with all the excitement surrounding the reopening of a central campus landmark. Despite not having much contact with its original partner USG, who, through regular turnover, no longer saw library textbooks as a policy objective worth devoting resources to over other affordability projects such as book-swaps and the promotion of open educational resources, the libraries did reach out and receive the USG's consent to relocate the project collection to the Thompson Library's closed reserve shelves.

A change in location also meant a big change in the project's functional parameters. Because it is not a 24-hour library, moving to Thompson Library eliminated overnight access to the collection. Folding the books into the closed reserve shelves further tightened access; in order to avoid confusion with other reserve materials, the project accepted the conventional two-hour loan term with the possibility of unlimited renewals unless another hold was placed on the item.

The cascade effects of these changes to the project were easily apparent. With an all but total drop in item theft and damage, the acquisition budget could be used to reliably grow the scope of the collection to cover more courses with more textbooks. In the years that followed, the adoption price floor was lowered to $50, minimum enrollment was adjusted down from 200 students to just 50, and the GEC courses of colleges outside of Arts and Sciences were considered to further expand the coverage map.

Moving from open to closed reserve also had beneficial effects for project assessment. Because each circulation transaction would now be recorded in the Millennium/Sierra catalog software, usage data could be collected and analyzed. A bit overzealous for statistics at first, the project began counting use every two weeks while in session along with a pre and post-finals snapshot of use each quarter; as the university transitioned from a quarter-based academic cycle to semesters in 2012, the data collection schedule was pared back to intervals immediately following the end of finals each term. The semester conversion included the university making a slight rhetorical change from "General Education Curriculum" to just "General Education"; as such the project also dropped the "C" to become the GE Textbook Project.

THE GE TEXTBOOK PROJECT TODAY: ANALYZING THE NUMBERS

The end of the 2016 spring semester marked the tenth full academic year that the libraries have been systematically involved in acquiring and loaning general education textbooks. Although it has undergone a substantial evolution during the past decade, what is now the GE Textbook Project retains its core mission: to provide undergraduate patrons with access to expensive required scholastic resources for general education courses. To that end, what follows is an examination of post-semester conversion practices and a look at some relevant assessment data.

Before peering into usage data, it may be useful to put the project's full expenditure over the last decade into perspective. Figure 9.1 provides basic figures concerning how much money was spent each fiscal year and how many items were purchased (excluding foundational acquisitions).

As it follows from the project's history, FY 2008 (and the first part of FY 2009) saw large expenditures and a higher average cost per item due to the burden of replacing multiple copies of the most expensive titles. FY 2010 and FY 2011 coincided with the project's relocation to the Thompson Library, and the steep drops in average cost per item during those periods can be attributed to the change in price floor, from $75 to $50, which accompanied expansion. Starting with FY 2012 the numbers become more stable; this represents the semester conversion and a new equilibrium for the project. Because the conversion elongated courses from 10 to 16 weeks, many departments and instructors recalibrated their textbook needs. This led to a large amount of content turnover for the renamed GE Textbook Project; rather than just the usual updating of editions, a considerable number of new titles were adopted to reflect longer syllabi. Fortunately for assessment purposes, using the conversion as a reflection point provides a glimpse into the rising costs of print textbooks (figure 9.2).

FISCAL YEAR	# OF ITEMS PURCHASED	TOTAL EXPENDITURE ($)	CHANGE (%)	EXPENDITURE PER ITEM ($)	CHANGE PER ITEM (%)
FY07	118	12,269		103.97	
FY08	146	22,196	80.91	152.03	46.22
FY09	86	14,573	34.34	169.45	11.46
FY10	74	9,913	-31.98	133.96	-20.95
FY11	143	15,560	56.97	108.01	-18.77
FY12	119	14,753	-5.19	123.97	13.94
FY13	117	14,603	-1.02	124.81	0.68
FY14	79	10,711	-26.65	135.58	8.63
FY15	87	11,832	10.47	136.00	0.31
FY16	67	10,437	-11.79	155.78	14.54

Figure 9.1 | **GE(C) Textbook Project Expenditures**

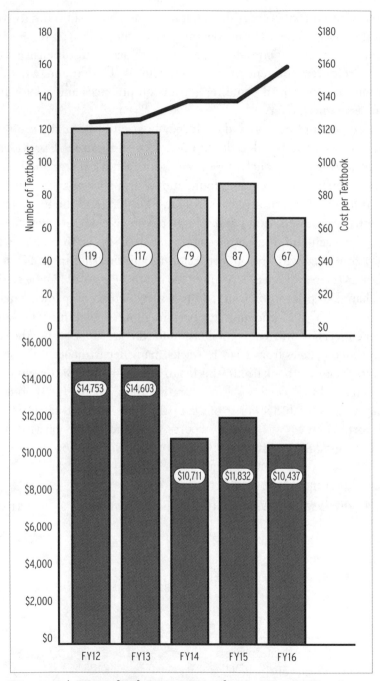

Figure 9.2 | **GE Textbook Project Expenditures FY2012-FY2016**

This general increase in the cost per item (represented by the line in the top graph) tracks well within the conventional wisdom surrounding textbook price inflation.

Another way to look at how print textbook prices have been changing can be to compare the price difference between various editions of the same title. As can be expected for a collection of this scope, the GE Textbook Project has purchased many updated or revised titles; figure 9.3 lists the average price increase between editions for disciplines that had at least one title adopted over multiple editions.

In analyzing figure 9.3, it should be noted that the largest increase (international studies) reflects a single title whose cost increased remarkably between its most recent editions; on the other end of the table, areas like math and accounting have experienced decreasing costs between editions. Because the data collected here refers to amounts that the library paid rather than the expected retail price of a given book, however, there is not enough statistical evidence to claim with certainty that these disciplines are seeing real massive increases or reductions in overall textbook prices. Instead, a relevant takeaway could be that, despite the rising clamor for affordability, the cost of print textbooks in general continues to outpace national inflation.

The large turnover in adopted titles that occurred during the semester conversion also triggered a spatial need for weeding. The guidelines for weeding the collection include removing from reserves titles that have ceased to be assigned for a course and editions of the same title that are two or more updates removed from the edition currently assigned (i.e., if the 13th edition of a textbook is adopted, both the 13th and 12th editions will be available on reserves while the 11th and older editions are removed). Removed items are most commonly transferred into the Thompson Library book stacks where they are allowed to circulate not only to Ohio State patrons, but also to any qualified user throughout the state's OhioLINK consortium. Some removed items, most notably those with damage or heavy duplication, are withdrawn per the libraries' regular monograph withdrawal process.

The usage of project items each semester has been high if statistically erratic, as seen in figure 9.4.

The material turnover that occurred with the semester conversion can also be a fruitful time stamp for another angle of usage assessment; tracking the items purchased for the collection in autumn 2012 offers a peek into how content fares within the GE Textbook Project. For that term, 93 new items representing 59 newly adopted titles were acquired at a cost of $12,028. Over

DISCIPLINE	MEAN INCREASE/EDITION (%)
International Studies	71.12
Agricultural Communication	59.76
History of Art	59.23
Linguistics	57.41
Engineering	55.29
Physics	45.52
Chemistry	43.38
Ag/Environmental/Developmental Economics	34.18
Astronomy	32.73
Sociology	32.64
Economics	32.13
Italian	29.99
Geography	28.99
Music	26.20
Social Work	25.59
English	24.55
Human Dev/Family Studies	23.98
Afro-American Studies	22.84
Earth Science	22.17
Anthropology	21.76
Statistics	21.43
Evol/Ecol/Org Biology	19.69
Biology	19.61
Kinesiology	19.09
Communication	16.56
Political Science	15.90
Consumer Science	9.56
French	6.32
History	6.10
Speech/Hearing	-2.67
Philosophy	-3.32
Molecular Genetics	-4.22
Psychology	-9.95
Mathematics	-11.02
Accounting	-18.99
Animal Science	-20.99
MEDIAN AVERAGE	22.05%

Figure 9.3 | **Average Price Increase between Consecutive Editions
of the Same Title by Discipline**

SEMESTER	NUMBER OF ITEMS	CHECKOUTS	CHANGE (%)
AU 12	479	4962	—
SP 13	514	4911	-1
AU 13	567	3663	-25
SP14	450	3934	7
AU 14	501	4400	12
SP 15	538	3034	-31
AU 15	525	3533	16
SP 16	550	2838	-20

Figure 9.4 | **GE Textbook Project Usage by Semester**

the next four academic years those items circulated 7,722 times; the median use per book is just above 33 with a low of one circulation, a statistics textbook, and a high of 755, a chemistry textbook. Factoring in each book's invoiced price finds a cost-per-use band that ranges from $0.13 to $140.75 with a median of $2.12 per use. Given the sheer size of the libraries' print monograph collection (almost 3,000,000 items), it should be no surprise that item use grades very high while cost-per-use grades very low vis-à-vis other circulating materials in the Thompson Library.

The above might make it appear that, due to the low use of the statistics textbook, the collection is not properly serving the students in the statistics discipline. If we look at usage based on broader categories of subject area, however, one can see that this is not necessarily the case. Figure 9.5 groups each covered discipline into one of seven greater areas.

As part of the broader "Math & Science" category, the Statistics Department is included in what is the largest share of use among textbooks. Furthermore, if we examine the top performing titles by the same categories (figure 9.6), it is a statistics title (*Statistics: Concepts and Controversies*) that comes in eighth overall in total use.

Some additional observations of the top five lists above include the popularity of foreign-language (Spanish and French) instructional textbooks within the Arts and Humanities area, the high relative use of education and human ecology textbooks and the low relative use of food, agricultural and environmental science (FAES) textbooks. Although there is, again, not enough statistical evidence to craft definitive declarations as to why certain materials circulate at a higher rate than others, it is worth noting that the departments of Spanish, French, and Human Development and Family Science all hold

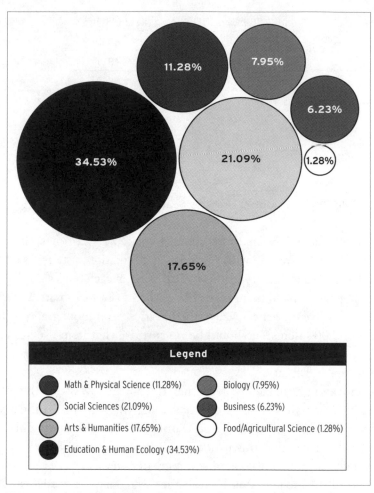

Figure 9.5 | **Share of GE Textbook Circulation by Subject Area**

classes on the university's central campus and each promotes the use of library textbooks to their students directly while OSU's FAES classrooms primarily reside over one mile away from the Thompson Library and are serviced directly by a department library nearby.

Even after ten years of project growth and change, questions remain regarding its effectiveness moving forward. Usage statistics can bolster the project's legitimacy within an academic library collection that primarily supports graduate and professorial research agendas, yet there continue to be some important institutional hindrances to maximum efficiency, while major changes to the textbook market itself may upend the entire concept of the printed textbook.

Arts and Humanities	1	Amistades	552
	2	Liaisons: An Introduction to French	508
	3	De Passeo: Curso Intermedio de Espano	429
	4	Gardener's Art Through the Ages	386
	5	A History of the Modern World	375
Biology	1	Campbell Biology	1727
	2	What is Life? A Guide to Biology with Physiology	1187
	3	Biology	693
	4	Human Biology: Concepts and Current Issues	75
	5	Biology: Concepts and Applications	17
Economics	1	Macroeconomics: Principles, Problems, and Policies	475
	2	Using Econometrics: A Practical Guide	468
	3	Concise Economic History of the World: From Paleolithic Times to the Present	322
	4	Principles of Microeconomics	282
	5	Macroeconomics	263
Education and Human Ecology	1	Marriages and Families: Making Choices in a Diverse Society	1237
	2	Infants and Children: Prenatal Through Middle Childhood	722
	3	The Process of Parenting	493
	4	Contemporary Nutrition	448
	5	Exploring Lifespan Development	426
Food, Agricultural, and Environmental Science	1	Animal Sciences	162
	2	Environmental Science for a Changing World	126
	3	Elements of the Nature and Properties of Solis	48
	4	Principles of Economics	41
	5	Anatomy and Physiology of Farm Animals	24
Math and Science	1	Chemistry: The Central Science	1806
	2	Vander's Human Physiology: The Mechanisms of Body Function	1726
	3	Calculus: Early Transcendentals	1327
	4	Statistics: Concepts and Controversies	743
	5	Physics	608
Social and Behavioral Sciences	1	Dynamics of Persuasion: Communication and Attitudes in	892
	2	A First Look at Communication Theory	764
	3	Our Origins: Discovering Physical Anthropology	717
	4	Psychology	518
	5	Cultural Anthropology	513

Sum of Checkouts broken down by Subject, Rank, and Title. The data is filtered on Date, which keeps 2011–12, 2012–13, 2014–15, and 2015–16. The view is filtered on Rank, which keeps 1,2,3,4, and 5.

Figure 9.6 | **Top Five Circulating Titles by Subject Area**

As was the case at the project's inception in 2006, identifying which materials are being adopted for each course every semester is very labor-intensive. The decentralized nature of campus bookstores and a culture wherein professors and departments interact directly with their chosen bookseller on adoption decisions means that no single proprietor holds a definitive list of adopted titles to share. At least a month prior to the start of each semester, the project staff begins combing over bookstore holdings, department websites, and edition publication cycles in an attempt to discern where new materials are likely to be adopted. In an effort to crowd-source that knowledge, in 2014 the project created a web-based "Suggest a Textbook" form that both students and faculty could use to let the libraries know about any course-adopted materials that the library did not currently hold; this has had very limited success, with only five textbooks being acquired directly from forms received. Even with foresight it is regrettably common for an adopted title to be unknown to the project until syllabi are released at the beginning of the semester, forcing last-minute rush acquisition that can stymie use as students who did not see the title in the library catalog settle on purchasing a copy from a bookstore.

Knowing, as G.I. Joe used to say, is half the battle. As the used textbook market and the growth of illegal digital access took profits away from traditional textbook publishing houses, those publishers found an impressive way to remain relevant in the Digital Age. Although e-textbook sales of popular titles still lag far behind their print equivalents, bundling either version of the textbook with online-only supplemental portals like Pearson MyLab & Mastering or McGraw-Hill Connect are forcing undergraduates back to paying high retail prices for required scholastic content.[4] Unfortunately for a university the size of Ohio State University, the library acquisition of e-textbooks and supplemental portal access is simply unaffordable; early in the GEC Textbook Project there was an attempt to pilot a multiuser e-textbook, but the publisher would not consent to the purchase of less than 700 individual licenses to reflect the number of available seats in the course. Likewise, the libraries cannot provide access to MyLab & Mastering or Connect due to the similarly unfavorable terms of these licenses.

Instead, the GE Textbook Project has refocused its outreach agenda not only to promote the print textbooks on reserve, but also to help patrons make sense of the rapidly changing paradigm. A recent partnership with a refocused USG and the university's Office of Distance Education and eLearning has created the Affordable Learning Exchange, which aims to better inform both students and faculty about all manner of affordable curricular materials, be they open access textbooks, curated electronic articles culled from library resources, or on-reserve print items. In this effort the libraries meet with textbook adopters to showcase library resources as an alternative to traditional textbooks and with students to discuss the GE Textbook Project and other legal methods to save money on scholastic materials.

CONCLUSION

Occasionally a well-meaning student or instructor will ask why the provision of general education textbooks at the library is called a project; after all, most things in academia that last over a decade become institutional. The GE Textbook Project moniker, however, remains as a rhetorical symbol that when it comes to maintaining a collection of adopted undergraduate textbooks in the twenty-first century, there can never really be complacency.

From its origins as a small, open reserve collection at OSUL's 24-hour library, the project has grown both up and out into a large, closed reserve collection housed within the campus's flagship library while also serving as a point of contact for the libraries' partners concerned with curricular content affordability issues. Missteps that occurred along the way were corrected when the project moved, allowing for growth in both size and scope and aiding in the development of better, if not best practices. These include the following:

- Establishing textbook price and course enrollment requirements that fit the institution and budget
- Keeping textbooks secure within a closed reserve system
- Holding the two most recent editions on reserve where possible
- Regular weeding of the collection to remove titles no longer assigned and editions twice removed from the currently adopted edition
- Tracking item use consistently on a semester-by-semester basis
- Preparing acquisition lists at least a month before the relevant term begins

The remaining challenges stem from institutional barriers that most large, public research universities face: privately owned bookstores and decentralized departments make the collection of timely adoption data a difficult and labor-intensive process, and emerging electronic curricular resources leave room for unworkable licensing situations. With usage that continues to impress and an overall university climate that favors any and all attempts to promote undergraduate affordability, however, there is little doubt that the GE Textbook Project will continue to grow and change while holding on to its foundational values.

Notes

1. Business Insider, "College Textbook Inflation Is Out of Control," blog entry by Mamta Badkar, April 24, 2014, www.businessinsider.com/textbook-price-inflation-2014-4.
2. Alan Woods, "Library to Provide GEC Textbooks," The Lantern, January 9, 2006, http://thelantern.com/2006/01/library-to-provide-gec-textbooks/.
3. Josh Zurn, "Vandalism Causing Problems to Library Textbook Program," The Lantern, March 9, 2009, http://thelantern.com/2009/03/vandalism-causing-problems-to-library-textbook-program/.
4. *Wall Street Journal,* "A Tough Lesson for College Textbook Publishers," blog entry by Josh Mitchell, August 27, 2014, www.wsj.com/articles/a-tough-lesson-for-college-textbook-publishers-1409182139.

Bibliography

Business Insider. "College Textbook Inflation Is Out of Control." Blog entry by Mamta Badkar. April 24, 2014. www.businessinsider.com/textbook-price-inflation-2014-4.

Wall Street Journal. "A Tough Lesson for College Textbook Publishers." Blog entry by Josh Mitchell. August 27, 2014. www.wsj.com/articles/a-tough-lesson-for-college-textbook-publishers-1409182139.

Woods, Alan. "Library to Provide GEC Textbooks." The Lantern. January 9, 2006. http://thelantern.com/2006/01/library-to-provide-gec-textbooks/.

Zurn, Josh. "Vandalism Causing Problems to Library Textbook Program." The Lantern. March 9, 2009. http://thelantern.com/2009/03/vandalism-causing-problems-to-library-textbook-program/.

ABOUT THE CONTRIBUTORS

POSIE AAGAARD is the assistant dean for collections at the University of Texas at San Antonio. She oversees departments that buy, manage, and provide access to the libraries' general collections. She leads negotiations for online collection agreements and helps advise faculty on scholarly communications issues, including copyright. Aagaard holds a certificate of advanced study in information systems and telecommunications management from Syracuse University and an MLS degree from the University of North Texas. She coauthored a 2015 article in *Reference Services Review* on the entrepreneurial uses of licensed databases.

KAY DOWNEY has been the collection management librarian for Kent State University (Ohio) since 2008. She also represents Kent State University Libraries at OhioLINK, the Ohio academic library consortium. Prior to her employment at Kent State University, she worked as serials and electronic resources librarian at the Ingalls Library, Cleveland Museum of Art.

JOANNA DUY is access services librarian at Concordia University Library (Montreal). Her previous positions at Concordia include head of access services (Vanier Library) and head of interlibrary loans and media services. Before coming to Concordia, she was a fellow and serials librarian at North Carolina State University Libraries in Raleigh. She holds an MLS degree from the University of Western Ontario and an MSc from Acadia University.

JOANNA EWING is the head of cataloging at the University of Central Arkansas' Torreyson Library in Conway, Arkansas. She graduated from the University of Alabama with a master's degree in library and information studies in 2006. In addition to cataloging, she actively participates in teaching library instruction sessions and providing reference services.

FENG-RU SHEU is currently an assistant professor and instructional design librarian for University Libraries at Kent State University (Ohio). Her research interests include applying learning theories, instructional approaches, and innovative technology to teaching and learning. She also advocates open education. Her research on open educational resources focuses on the impact of open textbooks that can be used freely, making higher education more accessible and affordable.

RHONDA GLAZIER is the director of collections management at the Kraemer Family Library, University of Colorado Colorado Springs. With over twenty-five years of experience in technical services, she has spent the majority of her time analyzing issues related to collection development, acquisitions, and the management of technical services. The subject of textbooks is especially interesting to her because of the intersection between circulation, library service, and technical services.

KIRSTEN HUHN is head of acquisitions and serials at the Concordia University Library (Montreal). Prior to coming to Concordia, she worked in technical services and interlibrary loan at Jacobs University in Bremen, Germany. A native of Germany, she holds an MA degree from Leipzig University and an MLIS from McGill University.

DUBRAVKA KAPA is the associate university librarian for research and graduate studies at Concordia University Library (Montreal). Her previous positions at Concordia include director of the Vanier Library and reference and subject librarian, and her responsibilities included the implementation of the textbook service. Her current professional interests include trying to think strategically and pragmatically about the future while having students, faculty, and the library in mind.

JAN H. KEMP is the assistant dean for public services at the University of Texas at San Antonio. She has previously held administrative positions at Texas Tech University and North Carolina State University. She is active in the Association of College and Research Libraries. Kemp has published articles in *College & Research Libraries, Journal of Academic Librarianship* (both 2015), *Journal of Electronic Resources Librarianship, Collection Management,* and others. She holds an MS degree in business administration from Texas Tech University and an MLIS from the University of Texas at Austin.

TOM KLINGLER is the assistant dean for systems, technical services, and collections at Kent State University (Ohio). He has experience in a variety of automation, collection, and consortium projects. He has taken a particular interest in recent years in the textbook dilemma.

RACHEL A. KOENIG is the instruction and assessment librarian and college archivist at SUNY Canton's Southworth Library Learning Commons. She earned her MLS degree from Indiana University and also holds an MA in history from Indiana University.

RENEE LeBEAU-FORD is presently the head of collection development at the University of Central Arkansas' Torreyson Library in Conway, Arkansas. LeBeau-Ford has been involved on campus in student success initiatives. She is also an instructor in the Library Media Program teaching reference services. She received her MLS degree in 1992 from San Jose State University in California.

CHRISTINE MCCLURE is the digital services coordinator for DePaul University in Chicago, where she directs web design, content, and digital service efforts. She performed the work discussed here while she was the digital services librarian for the Illinois Institute of Technology, also located in Chicago.

AMY MCCOLL is the assistant director for collections at Swarthmore College Libraries (Pennsylvania). She has been involved in the TriCollege Consortium and regional collaborative collection development projects for the past fifteen years, including shared print initiatives and collaborative approval plans. Her past experience includes stints as a cataloger, National Authority Cooperative Program coordinator, reference librarian, and archival assistant.

CARLA MYERS serves as the director of access services and scholarly communication for the University of Colorado Colorado Springs. In 2012 she launched the UCCS Copyright Education Initiative, through which she provides students and instructors with information on how protected works can be utilized for teaching, research, and scholarship. Her professional presentations and publications focus on fair use, copyright in the classroom, and library copyright issues.

AARON OLIVERA is currently the project coordinator for collection development at the Ohio State University Libraries. Since its inception in 2006, he has served as executor of the OSUL GE Textbook Project, which provides copies of course-adopted print textbooks to students via the libraries' reserves system. In this capacity he has spent the last decade working on myriad aspects of what is often referred to as "the textbook problem." He earned an MLIS from Kent State University.

PATTIE PIOTROWSKI is university librarian and dean of library instructional services for Brookens Library at the University of Illinois Springfield. In her previous position as assistant dean for public services at the Illinois Institute of Technology's Galvin Library, she worked to establish and enhance services for the faculty, staff, and students.

PEGGY SEIDEN has been college librarian at Swarthmore College (Pennsylvania) since 1998. Prior to joining Swarthmore, she directed the Skidmore College Library, the library at Penn State, and worked in various capacities at Carnegie Mellon University. Her research interests and publications are focused on user behavior and library organizational dynamics and collaboration. Her most recent publications include *Past or Portal? Enhancing Undergraduate Learning through Special Collections and Archives* (2012) which she coedited with Eleanor Mitchell and Suzy Taraba, and *Reviewing the Academic Library: A Guide to Self-Study and External Review* (2015), coedited with Eleanor Mitchell. Seiden is a past president of ALA's Reference and User Services Association and currently chairs the Choice Editorial Board. She has an MLIS degree from Rutgers University.

CORI WILHELM is the assistant director of library services and access services librarian at SUNY Canton's Southworth Library Learning Commons. She earned her MLS degree from University at Buffalo and also holds an MS in education from SUNY Potsdam.

INDEX